Written in Conjunction with the
Bicentennial of Wesley Chapel United Methodist Church
June 20, 2017

Sail on "Old Ship," nor fear the gales,
Our hopes and prayers will fill the sails,
Until thy sails at last are furled
In a new and ransomed world.

SAIL ON OLD SHIP

A History of
WESLEY CHAPEL
Floyd County, Indiana
1817-2017

By
Clifford. L. Staten, Ph.D.

Sail on Old Ship: A History of Wesley Chapel, Floyd County, Indiana: 1817-2017

Copyright © 2017 by Wesley Chapel and Clifford L. Staten. All rights reserved. No part of this publication may be reproduced, stored in a retrieval system or transmitted in any way by any means, electronic, mechanical, photocopy, recording or otherwise without the prior permission of the author except as provided by USA copyright law.

Published in the United States of America

Library of Congress Control Number 2017944796
Cataloguing data:
Clifford L. Staten
Sail on Old Ship: A History of Wesley Chapel, Floyd County, Indiana: 1817-2017
ISBN 978-0-9985592-5-4 (paperback ed.)

1. RELIGION / Church Institutions & Organizations
2. HISTORY / United States / State & Local / Midwest
3. RELIGION/Christianity/Methodist

Unless otherwise noted, all scripture references are taken from the Holy Bible, New International Version®, NIV®. Copyright © 1973, 1978, 1984, 2011 by Biblica, Inc.™ Used by permission of Zondervan. All rights reserved worldwide. www.zondervan.com Scripture quotations marked (NLT) are taken from the *Holy Bible, New Living Translation*, copyright © 1996, 2004, 2007, 2013, 2015, by Tyndale House Foundation, used by permission of Tyndale House Publishers, Inc., Carol Stream, Illinois 60188. All rights reserved. Scripture quotations marked (NASB) are taken from the *New American Standard Bible*® (NASB), Copyright © 1960, 1962, 1963, 1968, 1971, 1972, 1973, 1975, 1977, 1995 by The Lockman Foundation. Used by permission. www.Lockman.org.

The opinions expressed by the authors are not necessarily those of the publisher.

Published by Encourage Publishing, *LLC*
New Albany, Indiana 47150 USA
1-812-987-6148
info@encouragebooks.com
www.encouragebooks.com

Book design and layout by Encourage Publishing, LLC. All rights reserved.
Cover design by Leslie Turner
Interior design by Ahaa! Design + Production
Calligraphy by Connie Newbanks
Cover and title page photo by Todd Taggart Photography
Editing by Leslie Turner

Dedication

This brief history is dedicated to all who have served Him through Wesley Chapel since its founding on June 20, 1817.

Acknowledgments

A history such as this is the result of the efforts of many people, past and present, associated with Wesley Chapel United Methodist Church. These include Mrs. D.A. Smith, Katherine Cain, Mrs. Fred Jackson, Elizabeth Stoy, Fannie Wolf, Helen Bence, Irma Mae Hublar, Florence Mann, Hazel Long, Shirley Kendall, and Annette Gadlage. Bill Amerson provided a treasure trove of letters, photos, and materials that covered the entire history of Wesley Chapel. I am greatly appreciative of the substantive comments about the manuscript and the history of Wesley Chapel that he provided during several afternoon talks. This history would not have been possible without his assistance.

Reverend Tony Alstott provided important information, insights, and themes for the recent history of the church. Jim Ingram and Gina Wampler, the church secretary, also provided photos. Marcia and Steve Latimer, Jim Ingram, Dennis Reasoner, Diane Johnson, and my wife, Shannon Staten, were also helpful with their substantive comments and observations about the manuscript and our recent history. Over the past several years, many of our senior church members also provided invaluable information. Thanks to Connie Newbanks for her striking calligraphy that appears on the cover and in the text. I want to give Leslie Turner a very special thank you for her meticulous editing, her wonderful and insightful suggestions, and the care and love with which she approached this project. I want to thank Marcia Latimer for her leadership as chair of the Wesley Chapel Bicentennial Committee and the members of the committee for their hard work.

Finally, I want to thank Reverend Tony Alstott, who is providing the leadership for Wesley Chapel, the Old Ship, in its 3rd century as the members chart and follow a new course as a regional church in Floyds Knobs, Indiana

Table of Contents

FOREWORD 13

ABOUT THE AUTHOR 15

CHAPTER 1
Laying the Keel of the Old Ship 17

CHAPTER 2
Launching the Old Ship 27

CHAPTER 3
Enduring the Gale-Force Storms of Slavery
and the Civil War 35

CHAPTER 4
Navigating the Gilded Age 41

CHAPTER 5
Sailing into Headwinds:
The New Century, WWI, and the Roaring Twenties 49

CHAPTER 6
Surviving Hurricanes:
The Great Depression, the Flood of 1937, and WWII 55

CHAPTER 7
The Old Ship Journeys through Favorable Winds:
Post-WWII to the Mid-1960s 61

CHAPTER 8
Shifting Winds and Full Sail Ahead:
The Mid-1960s to 1998 69

CHAPTER 9
A Leap of Faith:
Charting a New Course and Setting Sail Again 77

    MINISTERS OF WESLEY CHAPEL 90

    ENDNOTES 92

Foreword

The frost covered the ground the last Sunday in November 2010 when Virginia Shannon arrived at Wesley Chapel on State Street at her regular time, just as she had faithfully done for so many years. It was a day of hope and opportunity for the future as well as for reflection on the past. It was the final service held at the State Street location. At the groundbreaking for the "new" Wesley Chapel held the previous Sunday, Virginia had symbolically turned the dirt at the new property just off Interstate 64 on Route 150. At that very moment, the sun broke through the overcast clouds and shone upon the congregation and the new site. It was an unmistakable sign to all that Wesley Chapel would continue to plot a clear and steady course for all who seek Him.

On this last Sunday on State Street, Virginia's thoughts raced from the promise of the future to the past. This day was not unlike the first Sunday in June 1964 when she attended the last service of the "downtown" West Market Street Wesley Chapel led by her husband, Pastor Lloyd Shannon. On that day, Wesley Chapel, having been at that location for 110 years, was getting ready to weigh anchor and set sail to State Street. While there were a few reservations about moving "way out" on State Street, Pastor Shannon, Virginia, and the congregation trusted the new course. This was yet reminiscent of another Sunday on December 31, 1854, when the final service was held in the original Old Ship as the members prepared to move to 202 West Market Street. Tradition states that the members of the congregation on that day "felt as though they were leaving home." Yet on that day, just as they would in the future, the members of Wesley Chapel would leave their home port and make sail to another so that they could continue to carry out the Great Commission to "go and make disciples of all nations."

Several themes are present throughout this brief history of Wesley Chapel United Methodist Church. From 1817 until 1964, it served as a local, community-based church in New Albany. After moving to State Street in 1964, it served as both a community-based and regional church. Since the move to its current location at I-64 and Highway 150 in 2013, Wesley Chapel has become a truly regional church serving and meeting the needs of its members and visitors from the entire "Kentuckiana" region, as the nearby Greater Louisville area and neighboring Southern Indiana counties have come to be collectively known. Wesley Chapel is the "Mother of Methodism" in New Albany and Floyd County. It was the first Methodist Church in the city and played a primary role in the creation of two other Methodist Churches. It also played a role in the establishment of other denominations in the area, and it has always cooperated with area churches.

Wesley Chapel has always been associated with education, whether it is creating educational institutions, having highly educated pastors, or watching many of its young members become ministers or go off to outstanding institutions of higher education. Lay leaders have always stepped forward to provide direction at critical times in the history of the church. These lay leaders have come from the very strong Sunday School education program that has been in place since the 1820s. Women, sometimes behind the scenes and other times out front, have always played a major role in the life and success of Wesley Chapel. More importantly, there is a long history of members reaching out and playing an active role in the missionary fields of the local community, the region, the country, and beyond the borders of the United States.

It should be noted that Wesley Chapel was originally a member of the Methodist Episcopal Church. The Methodist Episcopal Church, the Methodist Episcopal Church South, and the Methodist Protestant Church united to form the Methodist Church in 1939. The Methodist Church merged with the United Brethren Church to form the United Methodist Church in 1968. Wesley Chapel is typically referred to as a Methodist Church in this brief history.

About the Author

Clifford L. Staten, Ph.D.

Photo courtesy of Indiana University Southeast

Cliff Staten and his wife, Shannon, have been members of Wesley Chapel United Methodist Church since 1991. Both have served the church in many capacities. Cliff is a Professor of Political Science and International Studies at Indiana University Southeast in New Albany. He has written two books: The History of Cuba 2nd Edition (ABC-CLIO, 2015, original edition published in 2003) and The History of Nicaragua (ABC-CLIO, 2010) and published numerous scholarly articles on US foreign policy, Latin America, the presidency, and terrorism.

Laying the Keel of the Old Ship[1]

...and on this rock I will build my Church...
—Matthew 16:18

In the tradition of Jesus, the members of Wesley Chapel United Methodist Church have always been "fishers of men." For this reason, one must tell the history of Wesley Chapel within the context of the community and region it has served. The Church and the city of New Albany grew, developed, and changed together while weathering rough seas and sailing calm waters. New Albany, located west of the Falls of the Ohio River, was originally part of the George Rogers Clark land grant from the Virginia State Legislature. The Scribner brothers, Joel, Abner, and Nathaniel, who were from New York, founded the city. They purchased the land from Colonel John Paul of Madison, who had served under George Rogers Clark. Joel Scribner's son remembered that they landed at the foot of East Fifth Street. He recalled:

> There were occupied cabins in the place . . . The first ground cleared was on the south side of Main between Pearl and Bank on which four cabins were built . . . The surface of the new town presented a very uninviting appearance. The timber was very heavy, the undergrowth very thick, and the ground terribly uneven.[2]

They built a log cabin at the corner of East Sixth and Main Streets in 1813. John Kennedy Graham surveyed, laid out the town, and lots were sold the same year. The following year Joel and his wife, Mary, built the first framed house in the city at the corner of Main and State Streets.[3] The Scribner House, as it is known today, also served as the meeting place for the first Chamber of Commerce. The Chamber sent advertisements concerning the availability of land throughout the east including Pennsylvania, New York, Rhode Island, and Connecticut. One such advertisement read:

> The town, just laid out with spacious streets, public square, market, etc., is situated on the banks of the Ohio River at the crossing place from Louisville to Vincennes, about two miles below the Falls, in the Indiana Territory, affords a beautiful and commodious harbor.[4]

The city began to attract settlers. Steven Seabrook with his two sons, Daniel and James, arrived in 1814. Daniel Seabrook and his family played a major role in the early history of Wesley Chapel. The Wicks family from Erie, Pennsylvania arrived in 1816 with their daughter Mary, who became one of the pioneers of Wesley Chapel.[5] Another settler was a widower and Methodist from New Jersey, Harriet Reynolds, who had a ginger cake and spruce beer business in the front room of her house on the east side of Pearl Street just north of Main Street.[6] According to the traditional story:

> One bright moonlit evening in October 1816, Reynolds raised her voice to God and sang, "How tedious and tasteless the hours, when Jesus no longer I see." Elam Genung, [a blacksmith], who was taking a walk, heard Reynolds and stopped and entered the little cake shop. Reynolds stopped singing but Genung urged her to continue "that good old hymn" and joined her in the singing. Genung, also a Methodist, proposed the singing of another hymn and the offering of prayer. Several other people, including [Mary] Wicks, were attracted by the singing and also entered the little cake shop. A second prayer was led by Obadiah Childs who had come to New Albany with his sister, Elizabeth, from Maryland. This was the first religious service held in New Albany.[7]

A few weeks later Childs organized a weekly class meeting to provide Christian fellowship for all the Methodists in the town. Initially, there were 11 participants and Childs formed the class based upon the rules of the Methodist *Book of Discipline*. He opened a room for its meetings in his own home on the north side of Market Street just east of Bank Street. Childs' sister, Elizabeth, also participated in these meetings.[8]

On December 1 of the same year Indiana was admitted as the 19th state with Corydon as its capital. By that time, Methodism had already been established in the state and the effects of the religious revival and reform era called the Second Great Awakening were just becoming evident. The Second Great Awakening took place during the first half of the 19th century in the United States. Approximately one in 15 Americans attended church regularly in 1800. By 1850, one in seven Americans attended church regularly and 16 percent claimed church membership. The belief in "free will" rather than Calvinistic pre-destination fueled this religious resurgence. The concept of "free will" merged quite easily with the American belief in individualism and was a major tenet of the Methodist Church. Most of the new converts in America during this era were women. Its impact could be seen in the development of the movements for women's rights, temperance, and the abolition of slavery. L.C. Rudolph also points out that:

> Though the Catholics came to Indiana first, it was the growth of the Methodists which dominated the history of religion in the first half of the 1800s. Preaching is what made the Methodists… Preaching that was regular, frequent, and exciting…[9]

Early preachers, such as Samuel Parker and Edward Talbot, had come from Kentucky in 1801 and created a Methodist Society in Clark County. Nathan Robertson arrived in 1802 and visited settlements near Charlestown. In 1807, the Robertson Meeting House, "made of hewed logs" and sometimes referred to as the Old Bethel Church, was built on his farm. This was the first Methodist Church in Indiana.[10] The Silver Creek Circuit in the Clark Land Grant was established the same year with Moses Ashworth as the first circuit preacher. Ashworth was often referred to as the "Apostle of Methodism" in southern Indiana. The first Bishop of the American Methodist Church, Francis Asbury, visited Lawrenceburg as early as 1808 and played a major role in the rapid expansion of Methodism in Indiana and the country as a whole. Asbury emphasized what he called connectionalism and itinerancy. Connectionalism refers to the organizational structure and hierarchy, which unite all the Methodist Churches with a common governing structure and mission. Itinerancy refers to the rotating clergy who moved from settlement to settlement and were tied together through annual conferences. There were eight Methodist Circuits already established with a statewide church membership of 2,707 at the time of statehood in 1816.[11]

The following year New Albany was incorporated as part of Clark County while Childs continued to lead prayer meetings at his house. They were held on Wednesday evenings until the Reverend John Shrader officially organized the First Methodist Episcopal Society on June 20, 1817. Reverend Shrader gave the following account of the organization of Wesley Chapel:

The Reverend John Shrader[12]

I had heard with great pleasure and thankfulness to God, while assisting in a meeting at Gassaway's (then Bethel) near Charlestown, Clark County that a good work for Christ had been inaugurated at New Albany; and so I mounted my horse, on the morning of June 19, 1817 and rode over to New Albany. This was on Saturday.

I arrived in New Albany at noon and stopped at Hannah Ruff's tavern, over on the west side of State Street. I inquired for Obadiah Childs and was shown to his home. He soon gave me all the details of the work here, and insisted that I should stay over Sunday, hold a sacramental meeting, and organize a Methodist Society. We then went to Hannah Ruff's and asked her if we could use her dining room for the meeting on Sunday. She replied that we were welcome to the room. I went to my room in the tavern that night and prayed earnestly to God to be with me and help me in the work.

The sacramental meeting was held in the dining room of Hannah Ruff's tavern at two o'clock Sunday afternoon, June 20, 1817, when for the first time in New Albany, the sacrament of the Lord's supper was administered. Twenty-four persons took the elements of the broken body and shed blood of our Lord and Savior Jesus Christ. Then I proceeded to organize the Society, twenty-seven persons signing their names to the roll. It was a precious, as well as a historic, occasion - that organization of the first religious society in what is now Floyd County.

The next day, the members commenced to work for the erection of a church for themselves. The lot was procured, work commenced and pushed forward, and on November 25, 1817, I preached the sermon dedicating the church to the worship of Almighty God. By common consent, it was named Wesley Chapel. It was a high day for Methodism in New Albany.[13]

The first person to become a member was Elizabeth Brown Beeler, who remained a member for the next 78 years until her death.[14] The weekly class meetings during the winter of 1817-18 were held at the homes of Hannah Ruff on State Street and Obadiah Childs on Market Street because the original church was "neither lathed nor plastered." In other words, cold winds easily penetrated the rough walls. The membership grew to 18 people, consisting not only of heads of households but also young men and women. Most became faithful lifetime members of the church. They included Aaron Daniels and Peter Stoy, who were carpenters and had come to New Albany from Philadelphia, Henry Pitcher also from Philadelphia, and Edward Brown, Sr., who sold cattle and was originally from Baltimore.[15] Both sons of Aaron Daniels, William and John, became Methodist Ministers. Historian of early Methodism in Indiana and Pastor of Wesley Chapel, 1845-47, Fernandez C. Holliday, described Peter Stoy as one "whose influence was good" and was "represented by a pious posterity." The members of the Stoy family played leadership roles at Wesley throughout the 19th century. Other Methodists at that time included

Matthew Robinson, John Evans, Isaac Brooks, and Benjamin Blackiston. Robinson designed the first steamboat, the Volcano, and Daniel Seabrook helped to construct it in New Albany in 1817-18.[16]

The first Wesley Chapel Church was a 20-by-40-foot frame building located on Lafayette Street between Market and Spring Streets.[17] Construction began on June 21, 1817, and the first service was held on November 25 of the same year. The Scribner brothers donated the land, and George Evans, a carpenter, built it with materials donated by Thomas Sinex, Daniel Seabrook, and John Angell. Sinex, who became one of the first trustees of Wesley and whose son, Thomas, became a Methodist Minister, owned a lumberyard at Fifth and High (Main) Streets.[18] Seabrook, who also became a trustee of the church, made and provided oars and poles for flatboats and skiffs traveling down the Ohio River.[19] Angell was a class leader at Wesley for his entire adult life.

The Church had plank seats around the sides and one end of the building so that the older people could lean back against the walls in comfort. The other seats consisted of split logs with long wooden pins driven into the round part for legs. Henry McMurtrie referred to it simply as a "meeting house."[20] Isaac Reed described it "a little frame covered in."[21] Mary Wicks Stoy characteriized it as "a log structure of most unpretentious appearance," and the traditional history describes it as a "humble cabin of logs." Rather humorously, it was noted that it was not uncommon "for those that happened to fall asleep during the lengthy sermons to be suddenly awakened by a fall to the floor."[22]

There was plenty of work for Wesley Chapel in 1818. Life in the city was difficult, and most people could barely meet their physical needs, much less their spiritual ones. Isaac Reed, a Presbyterian Minister living in New Albany in 1818, stated, "As a place, its morals were low; its general society was rude, and much of it profane. There were some pious persons, but their numbers were small....The place had a sickly character."[23] Richard Lee Mason, who traveled through the town in 1819, described it as, "a little village inhabited by tavern keepers and mechanics."[24]

Reverend Shrader oversaw a four-week circuit in 1819. He preached at Wesley Chapel every fourth week. Class and prayer meetings were held the other three weeks. For a brief time in 1819, Presbyterians worshiped at Wesley Chapel because their church had burned.[25] Church membership reflected the growth of New Albany. In that same year, the city became the seat for the newly created Floyd County and had a population estimated to be 1,000, with approximately 150 wood frame houses and numerous log cabins. Boats that were traveling up the Ohio River had to wait in New Albany for high water so that they could get past the Falls of the Ohio, which acted as a natural barrier to river traffic. For seven months of the year, the city stood at the head of the "lower" Ohio River. With its strategic location, the growth of river traffic, and plenty of timber, iron ore, and hemp, the shipbuilding industry began to grow in New Albany. Three steamboats had already been launched from the growing shipbuilding industries located on the sloping land between Main Street and the river. Wesley Chapel attracted sailors from the riverboat traffic, and church membership stood at 67 in 1821.[26]

"The members of the Methodist Church in the town of New Albany met at the house of John Bodger on the evening of June 11, 1821, to elect trustees after having given a ten day notice as required [by Indiana law]."[27] Reverend Shrader acted as president, and Bodger served as clerk.[28] The following were elected as the first Trustees of Wesley Chapel: Thomas Sinex, Benjamin Blackiston, Edward Brown, Sr., Robert Downey, and Peter Stoy, who was married to the former Mary Wicks.[29] They were elected "for the purpose of receiving any donations that may be made to church." Other members included Barbara Downey, Maria Beeler, William Beeler, Elizabeth Beeler, Mary Wicks Stoy (wife of Peter Stoy), Hannah Ruff, Eliza Blaskiston (wife of Benjamin Blackiston), Flora Sinex (wife of Thomas Sinex), John Evans, John Strange, Obadiah Childs, Elizabeth Childs Turner (sister of Obadiah Childs and wife of Captain Henry Turner), Mary Sigler Pennington, Ann McClarey Brooks, Samuel Beeler, and Mary Beeler.[30]

A Sunday School was created in 1823-24 and met in the New Albany Court House. Edward Brown, Sr., of Wesley Chapel, was the first Superintendent.[31] Methodists, Baptists, and Presbyterians attended until 1829, when Wesley created its own Sunday School with 70 students and 12 teachers.[32] By 1839-40, Sunday School attendance had reached 250 to 300 students each week.[33] This tradition of excellence in Sunday School education continues to this day.

By 1826, the members realized that the small frame church on Lafayette Street was simply too small to meet the growing needs of Wesley Chapel. On October 18, the Trustees, Edward Brown, Sr., Benjamin Blackiston, Peter Stoy, Dorman Smith, and Obadiah Childs, purchased a 60-by-100-foot lot on the southeast corner of Market and First Streets for $81.[34] In 1827, a one-story brick building of about 35 by 50 feet was built. The Reverend George Armstrong donated the foundation timbers. "The front was about 40 feet back from the street with a large yard in front enclosed with a high, open fence having a fancy gate with a high, circular top."[35] Upon completion of the new building, traditional history provides commentary as to how it became known as "the old ship:"

> What a source of satisfaction and comfort it must have been for the congregation, who had been meeting in the crowded, unplastered church on Lafayette Street, to meet in the new, comfortable, and commodious brick church. They laid their plans broad and deep for the Lord; they made sacrifices to carry them out; they lived frugally and saved that they might give to the Lord, and He accepted their offerings. Much, yes, very much, of the subsequent welfare, prosperity, and morality of New Albany is due to the self-sacrificing men and women comprising this early Methodist Church. In 1833 or 1834, a 15-by-50 foot wing was added on each side of the original structure, making the building 65 by 50 feet. It was at this time that the steamboat men, many of whom attended there when home, named the church The Old Ship of Zion. "For," said they, "she has her wings spread and is ready to sail away."[36]

City and church traditions came together in 1829 with the placement of the bell in the cupola of the courthouse. Citizens held a watch service each New Year's Eve, with all in prayer for the upcoming year. At midnight, the courthouse bell would ring, and all would sing "God Be with You Till We Meet Again." By this time, the Old Ship, or Wesley Chapel, had become one of the most important churches, a "rock" in the Indiana

Methodist Conference. It had 282 members as of 1831 and was the site of the organization of the Indiana Conference of the Methodist Episcopal Church on October 17, 1832, which was presided over by Bishop Joshua Soule. Sixty Methodist Ministers received appointments on that day, and it was reported that there were 31,058 people who were members of the church in Indiana.[37] This coincided with the beginning of the phenomenal growth of the city of New Albany as the steamboat and shipbuilding industry prospered. At the same time, the Old Ship was poised to set sail and play a major role in the development of the city, its people, and Methodism in New Albany and Indiana.

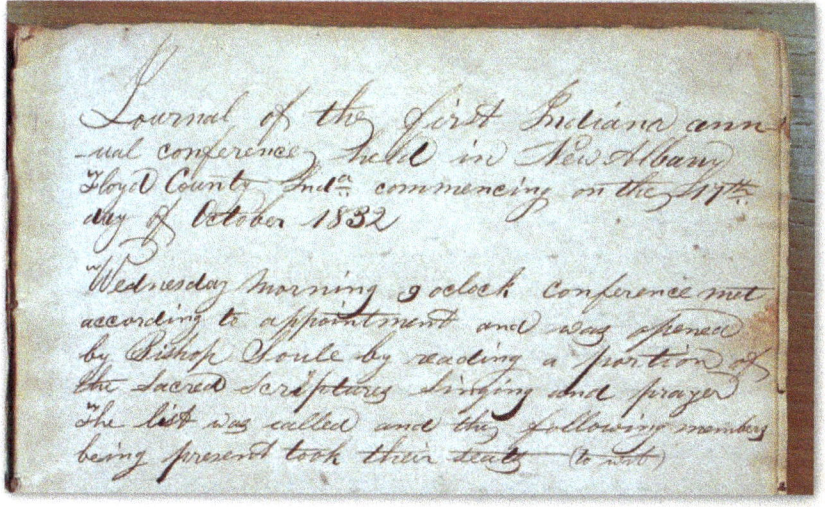

Photo Copy of the Journal of the First Indiana Annual Conference of the Methodist Episcopal Church, held in New Albany at Wesley Chapel, October 17, 1832. Courtesy of the Indiana Conference.

Launching the Old Ship

…they continued to meet together…praising God…
And the Lord added to their number daily…
Acts 2:46-47

From 1830 to 1860, the population of New Albany grew from a little more than 2,000 to more than 12,500 people. It was officially designated a city in 1839 and become the largest city in the state by 1850. Business with the southern states fueled the growth of the steamboat and shipbuilding industries as well as supporting trades such as machine shops, cabinet and furniture factories, copper and silversmiths, glass and iron works, and foundries. Between 1847 and 1867, more than 204 steamboats were built in New Albany. Five shipyards employed more than 200 skilled mechanics. Large, stately homes, which still stand today, were built along Market Street. In 1847, a railroad line was established between New Albany and Salem. In 1853, the first public high school in the state of Indiana, New Albany High School, opened. In 1859, the Governor of Indiana, Ashbel P. Willard, who lived in New Albany, dedicated the Floyd County Fairgrounds, where the State Fair would be held. The city was very wealthy by the beginning of the Civil War. More than one-half of all Hoosiers making more than $100,000 per year lived in New Albany.[38]

Growth, prosperity, and development also came to Wesley Chapel. Members decided to build an educational institution because "many of its own members had never received a formal education." In 1835, the church purchased the adjoining lot of 60 x 100 feet on the east side and built a 60 x 40 frame building which became the New Albany Methodist Seminary.[39] The building had two rooms downstairs and one large room upstairs. The following members of Wesley Chapel played the primary role in the establishment of the seminary: "Ruter, Wiley, Sinex, Leonard, Brown, Downey, Robinson, Evans, Stoy, Childs, Conner, and Seabrook."[40] The seminary, which came under control of the Indiana Conference in 1837, was a cross between a senior high school and a junior college. Hundreds of students passed through its doors. Marcus Ruter and the Reverends W.H. Goode and George H. Harrison served as principals of the seminary. Reverend Harrison was a graduate of Augusta College and was considered "a teacher of rare abilities."[41] The seminary had 200 students with two male and two female teachers in 1837 under the leadership of W.H. Goode.[42]

Graduates who later became preachers included Charles Downey, John W. Locke, Thomas H. Sinex, George B. Jocelyn, and Thomas G. Beharrell. Sinex became a college professor and the first president of Albion College and president of the University of the Pacific, Jocelyn became the second President of Albion College, Locke became a mathematics professor at DePauw and president of three different universities, and Beharrell became a noted author. John W. Locke's daughter, Betty, was a member of the first group of females to be admitted to DePauw University in 1867.[43] While the seminary closed in 1843, largely due to issues of debt, it laid the foundation for the creation of the Indiana Asbury Female Seminary by the Indiana Methodist Conference at East Ninth and Main Streets which opened in 1852.[44] The seminary "prepared daughters of well-to-do families" of the region but fell into debt due to declining attendance during the Civil War. Washington C. DePauw paid the debts of the seminary in 1866 and the seminary was renamed the DePauw College for Young Ladies. It eventually closed in 1908.[45]

From 1817 to 1838, the Pastors of Wesley Chapel included Peter Cartwright, W. H. Goode, George Locke, Samuel Lowe, William McReynolds, William Shanks, John Shrader, John Strange, James Thompson, Calvin W. Ruter, and Allen Wiley.[46] All of these exceptional men were circuit riders. Methodist clergy members were assigned to a circuit or charge in a geographic region. Each circuit had at least two churches or stations for which the minister was responsible. Ministers traveled from one church to the next in the circuit while preaching the Gospel and meeting the needs of the church members. Fernandez C. Holliday described Shrader as having "such energy, devotion, and toil, such cheerful self-denial and unostentatious moral heroism…[he] has never been equaled in the history of our Church." Cartwright was a "natural orator" and a "diamond in the rough." Locke and Wiley were "great preachers." Locke preached "like a man who felt he was moved upon by the Holy Ghost." Strange, the "prince of circuit riders," had a talent for "witty sayings." He was popular, had a "powerful voice," and his "sermons were highly descriptive." Ruter "possessed a strong and clear voice." Wiley, a Latin and Greek scholar, who served at Wesley Chapel in 1836, was meticulous in keeping a map of the city with all the residences of his members noted. He visited these families at least once every three months. His preaching was "lengthy" and "rich in thought and profound in argument." Holliday suggests that Wiley "perhaps more than any other man, molded the character of Indiana Methodism."[47]

The Indiana Methodist Conference was held in New Albany in October 1837 with Bishop Joshua Soule presiding. Reverend John C. Smith, an abolitionist, became Pastor of Wesley Chapel in 1838 and led a revival which swept through the city. John Parsons, who visited New Albany at that time, described it in his diary as a "most extensive and powerful revival of religion."[48] Peter R. Stoy described it as "one of the most powerful and far-reaching in its influences ever known" and he pointed out that "the converts were from all classes of society."[49] Meetings were held day and night for several weeks and hundreds were saved and became members.[50] As a result, the Church, now with 943 members, once again needed more space. The Trustees decided to build a new church "uptown." Centenary Church was built in 1839. Both congregations remained members of Wesley Chapel for two years. They were served by Pastors W.V. Daniel and Silas Rawson from 1840 to 1842. The property and membership were divided and each became a separate organization in 1841. The Old Ship had literally launched a new Methodist Church in New Albany.[51]

Several members of Wesley Chapel served New Albany after its designation as a city in 1839. Edward Brown, Sr., one of the first trustees, served as the city's first treasurer 1839-44. Thomas Sinex, also one of the first trustees, served on the city council 1843-45, and Obadiah Childs, one of the founding members and an early trustee, served as city collector 1848-50. Edward Brown, the son of Edward Brown, Sr., served on the city council 1839-40 and Peter R. Stoy, the son of founding members Peter and Mary Wicks Stoy, also served on the city council 1850-51.

By this time, the second generation of the founding members of Wesley Chapel began to play an active role in the church. Peter R. Stoy became the superintendent of Sunday School in 1843 and served periodically in that position for the next 40 years.[52] He married Ellen Beeler, the daughter of William and Elizabeth Beeler, also founding members of Wesley Chapel, who taught Sunday School the remainder of her life. Anne Marie Seabrook, the daughter of Daniel Seabrook, who had supplied materials for the first church building and was an early trustee of the church, taught Sunday School for more than 50 years. Mary Wolfe Seabrook, Daniel Seabrook's daughter-in-law, played the church organ.

Revivals continued in New Albany throughout the 1840s and early 50s. The following Pastors led the Old Ship from 1842 to 1854: George C. Beeks (1842-43), Enoch Woods (1843-45), Fernandez C. Holliday (1845-47), James Hill (1847-49), W.C. Smith (1849-50), Hiram Gilmore (1850-52), and James H. Noble (1852-54). The sermons of Enoch Woods were "instructive" and "argumentative" in style.[53] Reverend Woods presided over the mass funeral held at Wesley for the more than 100 people who perished in the explosion of the riverboat, Lucy Walker, on the Ohio River just south of New Albany wharf on September 23, 1844 and a year later presided over the funeral of Peter Stoy, one of the founding members of Wesley Chapel. The scholarly Holliday went on to become one of the noted historians of early Methodism in Indiana. Reverend James Hill, who later received a Doctor of Divinity degree from DePauw, was a "preacher of great power and popularity and a most successful soul-winner." He had a passion for revivals and, according to Dr. J.M. Caldwell, he was "one of the great men of our ministry, whose work has made Methodism a success in this country."[54] Reverend W.C. Smith had a "popular" preaching style.[55]

During the 1830s and 40s, slavery became a critical national issue that also divided the Methodist Church. At the Methodist General Conference held in Louisville in 1844, the south broke away from the Methodist Episcopal Church and created the Methodist Episcopal Church South. An anti-slavery group from the Methodist Episcopal Church of Portland, Kentucky petitioned for and was annexed to Wesley Chapel in 1846. While this helped to increase the anti-slavery membership at Wesley Chapel, it was just one example of how divisive the issue of slavery had become. The slavery issue was evident in the support or lack of support for the Mexican-American War of 1846-48. The Methodist Episcopal Church South supported the war largely because of the possibility of adding slave states to the union, whereas the Methodist Episcopal Church, now representing the north, was very critical of the ties between the war, expansionism, and slavery.[56]

The Indiana Conference was held in New Albany in 1848 and membership at Wesley Chapel stood at 390 people.[57] The history of Wesley Chapel during this time also reflected internal debates over music that are strikingly familiar to members today. The following, rather amusing passage, illustrates the debates concerning whether singing should reflect the traditional or "new-fangled" music and where the choir should stand in church.

> ...the question as to the means of improving the singing engaged the attention of the Official Board. Up to that time the plan had been for some good brother or sister to start the tune and the congregation joined in the singing of the hymn, the preacher reading it out two lines at a time. The time had now come, however, when churches were agitated over organs and choirs; there was much opposition to their introduction, many old members not consenting to this "new-fangled singing;" but progress was the order of the day, and both the choir and organ were finally introduced into Wesley Chapel.
>
> The first choir was organized in the Old Ship about the year 1851, with Benjamin Deacon as leader. The proper place in the church for the choir seemed an uncertain and delicate question. In the present auditorium, their place was in the center of the room; afterwards, they were moved to the gallery; from thence to the "amen" corner on the left hand side; and from there to the rear of

the room. With this last move, one of the members of the Official Board offered a motion that the choir be placed on wheels.[58]

By 1850, the city's population had nearly doubled since 1839 to 8,181 residents. The Old Ship had reached its capacity again. More than 200 members were sent to create Robert's Chapel, which is now Main Street United Methodist Church, but at that time was often called the "Yawl" in reference to the Old Ship. The Old Ship had now launched a second Methodist Church in New Albany. A visitor to the Old Ship, the Yawl, and Centenary in 1852 commented that they "appear to be prosperous and increasing in usefulness and piety. The congregations are large and attentive and afford evidence of a high appreciation of the services rendered them by a pious, talented, and faithful ministry."[59]

The Old Ship, Centenary, the Yawl, and other churches held many temperance meetings from 1852 through 1854 according to Maria Graham, a teenager and daughter of John Kennedy Graham. John Kennedy Graham was a teacher, lawyer, engineer, a member of the Indiana House of Representatives and the Senate, a member at the Indiana Constitutional Convention, and the original surveyor of New Albany. Maria Graham indicated in her diary that "reformed drunkards" often spoke to the youth at several churches in the city. At one particular meeting on March 2, 1854 at Wesley Chapel, Milton Gregg, the editor of the *Tribune*, and "Mr. Echols" of Virginia spoke to them about the problems associated with drinking. She also noted that there were lectures on matrimony and the evils of tobacco. Graham specifically referred to Wesley Chapel as the Old Ship and wrote that she also attended the last sermon of Pastor Noble on September 26, 1854.[60]

The congregation discussed the question of the necessity for a larger building in 1853. N.H. Cobb, Samuel Parker, Christian Tilson, William Lynn, E.R. Day, George Payne, F.A. Hutchinson, Samuel Marsh, John McBride, Daniel Seabrook, and Peter R. Stoy held a meeting and completed the initial arrangements on June 9. The lot at 202 West Market Street was bought in the fall of 1853 for $1,500 and work on the building began in the spring of 1854.[61] According to tradition:

Care was exercised in the laying of the foundation. More than 50 barrels of cement, a rare material in New Albany up to that time, were used. The walls were built very heavy and solid with more than 532,000 hard bricks. The Sunday School class rooms of the new building were completed by the end of December 1854.[62]

The Indiana Conference was held in New Albany in September. The final service held in the Old Ship was on the last Sunday of 1854. At that time, Reverend J.Y. McKee (1854-56) was serving as Pastor of Wesley Chapel. According to tradition:

It was a very solemn occasion and all felt as though they were leaving home. The only parts of the old Church used in the new building were the old seats which were transferred to the class rooms and the altar which was placed in the Sunday School room. The building was used for the first time on the first Sunday of 1855. The same order of seating was observed as in the old Church, the males on one side and the females on the other. Under no circumstances were they permitted to sit together. These restrictions continued until the main audience room was dedicated, when a few families dared to break the rule and sit together. The main audience room was completed in September 1855 and the new Church was dedicated to the service of Almighty God on the second Sunday in November 1855 by Dr. [David Wasgatt] Clark who later became Bishop and Reverend [James B.] Finley. The cost of the structure, including the lot and furniture, totaled $19,164.56. The old Church property had been sold in the spring of 1854 for more than $7,000, and this together with the subscriptions received, left only $800 to be raised on dedication day.[63]

The *New Albany Daily Ledger* reported that there were 1,300 people present at the dedication. It was described as a "plain and neat structure, built more for convenience than beauty." The sanctuary was located on the second floor while the Sunday School auditorium and classrooms were at street level. Wesley Chapel, the Old Ship and the Mother of New Albany Methodism, had launched two new churches and at least one school. It now stood at its new location on West Market Street, but members would soon be confronted with a storm of monumental proportions.

Enduring the Gale-Force Storms of Slavery and the Civil War

It is no fault in others that the Methodist Church sends more soldiers to the field, more nurses to the hospitals, and more prayers to heaven for the preservation of the Union, than any other. God bless the Methodist Church – bless all the churches – and blessed be to God, who, in this our great trial, giveth us the churches.

President Abraham Lincoln • May 18, 1864

President Lincoln and Chief Justice Salmon P. Chase clearly recognized the importance of the Methodist Church in its tremendous support of the Union and the Republican Party, especially in the lower Midwestern states of Indiana, Illinois, and Ohio.[64] While Indiana had been admitted into the United States as a free state and its constitution forbade slavery, most of the people in New Albany were sympathetic to slavery, and some residents owned slaves. This was because the shipbuilding industry depended on business contacts in the south and many who lived in New Albany were originally from slave-holding states.

The editor of the New Albany Daily Ledger from 1855 to 1869, John Norman, was a "strong foe of abolitionism and notorious for his constant degradation of African-Americans."⁶⁵ He used the paper to fuel proslavery public opinion in the city, spreading fear among New Albanians that abolition would bring a flood of African-Americans in, who would compete with white laborers and thereby lower their wages.. The Young Men's Christian Society attempted to bring the famous New England abolitionist, Wendell Phillips, to New Albany for a lecture in 1856, but the event was cancelled due to the controversy that it caused among the people.

Yet, as with most towns in southern Indiana along the Ohio River, there were those who opposed slavery. The Methodists, who were the largest religious denomination in New Albany and Floyd County, generally opposed slavery. Abolitionist preachers spoke at several of the Methodist, Presbyterian, and Baptist Churches. Reverend Benjamin F. Crary, a graduate of Pleasant Hill Academy (Belmont College), had been a schoolteacher, a lawyer, and later became President of Hamline University. Reverend Crary who served as Pastor of Wesley 1856-57, was one of the first supporters of the anti-slavery Republican Party and most outspoken in his condemnation of the evils of slavery and the fugitive slave laws. He preached against slavery on Sundays, offered letters to the local newspapers, and urged that the Discipline of Methodism be changed to exclude from membership anyone who owned slaves. Former Wesley Chapel Pastor and abolitionist, John C. Smith (1838-40), offered a resolution at the October 1857 Indiana Methodist Conference held in New Albany to deny membership in the Church to anyone who owned slaves. The Conference voted to pass the resolution, due in no small part to the passionate debating skills of Crary. The New Albany Daily Ledger criticized Crary and other anti-slavery preachers, referring to them as "political" preachers.⁶⁶ Crary was later described as "too radical to be popular."⁶⁷ The Reverend Daniel A. Payne, Bishop of the African Methodist Episcopal Church and noted abolitionist, spoke at Wesley Chapel, as did the famous abolitionist and Presbyterian Preacher Henry Ward Beecher the following year in 1858.

Lay leaders of Wesley Chapel in the mid-1850s included F.A. Hutchinson, John McBride, Michael Streepy, William Lynn, Samuel Parker, Joseph Armstrong, J.C. Davis, John Angell, Benjamin Deacon, and Jacob Wall. Recording stewards included J.G. Harrison, C.E. Jones, Michael Streepy,

Pastor Benjamin F. Crary, Wesley Chapel 1856-57. Courtesy of Stuart B. Wrege Indiana History Room, New Albany-Floyd County Public Library.

and Peter R. Stoy.⁶⁸ Streepy also served as the New Albany City Treasurer (1855-56). Samuel Reed (1857-58) and S.B. Sutton (1858-60) served as Pastors of Wesley Chapel in the immediate years preceding the Civil War. Reed was described as "a queer, half-way-mystic spiritualist" and Sutton as "fairly well distinguished."⁶⁹ The Indiana Conference, held in New Albany in September of 1857, determined who would pastor The Old Ship as the Civil War loomed. Throughout 1860 and early 1861, most of the talk in the church and the city focused on the possibility of civil war. During this time, John M. Green (1860-62) served as pastor. Traditional history states that Pastor Green made a salary of $600 per year.

By 1860, New Albany's population of 12,647 was five percent African-American, possibly the highest percentage among all cities in Indiana.[70] Most were freed slaves and lived in the West Union neighborhood north of Falling Run Creek. These individuals played a pivotal role in the Underground Railroad.[71] The Anti-Slavery League of Indiana had placed boats and skiffs along the Ohio River to assist runaway slaves, who had been crossing the Ohio River to New Albany as early as 1821. Runaway slaves often used the railroad that ran from New Albany to Salem. The influx of escaping slaves into New Albany during the Civil War led to increased violence toward African-Americans and arrests of slaves. A group of whites attacked African-Americans as they were having a picnic and a dance in August 1860. Many African-Americans were warned to leave New Albany after the incident.

Sketch of New Albany in 1861. The Ohio River is on the right and Portland is across the river in Kentucky.[72]

Hayden Hays (1862-64) served as pastor of Wesley Chapel as the Civil War entered its second year. A race riot broke out on July 22, 1862, where many acts of violence and vandalism were committed against the city's

African-American community. The 30-hour riot ended after military patrols appeared on the streets.[73]

The city of New Albany served as a gathering point for Union troops heading south, a strategic supply center for Union armies fighting in the south, and a hospital center for wounded soldiers being sent north. In fact, there were three military hospitals in the city, including one for African-American soldiers. President Lincoln established a National Cemetery in the city in 1862. While there were no battles fought in New Albany, a Union gunship from New Albany unsuccessfully attempted to prevent Confederate raiders led by General John Hunt Morgan from crossing the Ohio River at Brandenburg, Kentucky, into Indiana near Corydon.[74]

During the war, all church meetings were suspended, except Sundays. Church members held class and prayer meetings at their homes. The Second Presbyterian Church, now the Second Baptist Church, served as a station on the Underground Railroad in New Albany. While many Methodists were involved in the Underground Railroad, it must be noted that little is known of the activities of Wesley Chapel during the Civil War because its records were lost in the 1937 flood.

James H. Noble (1864-67) was serving as pastor of Wesley Chapel as the Civil War drew to a close. Sunday School attendance stood at 240 to 275 students each week during the pastorate of Reverend Noble.[75] In 1866, a new music hall opened in New Albany. It was considered one of the finest in the Midwest and could seat 2,500 people. Pastor Noble, who had also served at Wesley from 1852 to 1854, opposed attendance at the opening of the new Music Hall. He spoke of the "immorality" of attending these public performances.[76] Dr. John Poucher, a member of Wesley as a youth, a graduate of DePauw University and Garrett Biblical Institute, a Methodist Minister, and a professor at DePauw, noted in his address at the centennial celebration of Wesley Chapel in 1917 that just after the Civil War, when Noble was Pastor, Wesley Chapel's choir director was Ben Deacon. He also remarked that a female, Annie Cross, served as the Church organist. Dr. Poucher and Annie Cross would later marry.[77] The Indiana Conference was held in New Albany in September of 1865, during Noble's second year, to assign itinerant pastors for the next cycle.

Reverend William McKendree Hester, a graduate of DePauw University, served as Pastor from 1867 to 1870. He was "friend, counselor, and helper of all of the flock, and endeared himself to all by his loving, sympathy, and care." His sermons "evinced painstaking preparation."[78] With the Civil War finally at an end, the city of New Albany had to adapt to the declining steamboat industry, which had dominated the city in its early years. The stage was set for the Old Ship to navigate the era of industrialization and the decades of steep political and social changes that would follow.

Navigating the Gilded Age

And with a pillar of cloud You led them by day, and with a pillar of fire You led them by night to light the way in which they were to go.
NEHEMIAH 9:12 (NASB)

The Civil War ended the steamboat era of New Albany because so much of its business with southern states had come to an end. The last steamboat, the Robert E. Lee, was finished in 1870, and it marked the end of the "antebellum boomtown." Yet with its somewhat prosperous and mostly native-born skilled workers, New Albany was transformed into a factory town of iron, plate glass, and woolen mills dominated by Washington C. DePauw. His American Plate Glass Company operated in New Albany from 1865 to 1893 and employed as many as 2,000 people. By 1870, the iron and plate glass industry combined to produce more than one million dollars of product and a growing trade union movement.[79]

While looking beyond the pain of the Civil War, the church continued to maintain its bonds to the early years of New Albany, under the leadership of Stephen Bowers (1870-71). Even the pulpit furniture in the sanctuary in the 1870s hearkened back to the beginnings of the Old Ship. Belonging to Wesley's first pastor, John Shrader, it consisted of five cathedral chairs, the pulpit, a marble-top table, and two pedestals, all of walnut and beautifully hand-carved.[80] Reverend Bowers, who served as Chaplain with the 67th Indiana Infantry Volunteers during the Civil War, gave many temperance lectures and "often mixed religion and politics."[81]

Reverend Stephen Bowers[82]

Wesley Chapel continued to be a periodic host of the Indiana Conference, as it did again in 1871. That same year, the Women's Foreign Missionary Society was established at Wesley with 28 members. This society provided both an opportunity to learn about other countries and a service opportunity for women. Its purpose was to encourage its members to pray for and raise funds to minister to women missionaries in foreign countries. According to the organization's minutes, the religions of China, Africa, Russia, and Persia were often discussed. Early leaders of this group included Sue Hooper, Anne Mitchell, Hattie Beeler, Elizabeth Stoy, Emma Heart, and Annie Bullock. Pastor Bowers left Wesley in 1871 and went west to Oregon and then California, where he became an amateur archaeologist.[83]

Reverend Aaron Turner (1871-72) took over the pulpit upon Bowers' departure. Reverend Turner, "a man of attractive presence," was most personable and described as a preacher who "stood at front rank." He also was known as an excellent singer.[84] Under Pastor Turner in 1871, the Sunday School classes made a sizeable donation to the victims of the Great Chicago Fire.[85] He presided over the funeral of Elizabeth Childs Turner, one of the founding members of Wesley Chapel and wife of the late Captain Henry Turner.[86]

Joseph Shell Woods (1872-74) had the wheel when a deep economic downturn gripped the city. The depression of 1873-79 led to strikes in New Albany that were opposed by the entire elite establishment: the city newspaper, the Ledger Standard, city leaders, business leaders (especially DePauw), the leaders of both the Democratic and Republican Parties, and church leaders. Unemployed workers and those on strike often held "Have Nothing" carnivals filled with plenty of singing and drinking while they wore ragged clothes to mock the depressing conditions and made fun of politicians and businessmen.[87]

Several members of Wesley Chapel were considered part of the prominent leadership of New Albany at this time. Peter Raymond Stoy, son of one of the founding families of Wesley, was the General Manager, Vice President, and Treasurer of DePauw's Ohio Falls Iron Works. He had to deal with a strike that lasted several months in 1874 after the company imposed a two percent wage cut on all the workers. Stoy had regularly served on the City Council since the early 1850s, and his sons, Lewis and Raymond, ran his very successful hardware business. Frederick D. Conner was the Assistant Secretary and Director of the New Albany Forge and Rolling Mill, and James G. Harrison was a Trustee of the DePauw College for Young Women, a Trustee of the city schools, and the Deputy United States Clerk and United States Commissioner for the federal court in New Albany. He was the son of the Reverend George H. Harrison, who served as Principal of the New Albany Methodist Seminary in the early 1840s.[88] By 1876, during the tenure of Reverend W.H. Grim (1874-77), membership at Wesley stood at 385, and the first pipe organ was installed in the church the following year.[89]

Reflecting the elitist and sometimes racist sentiments of New Albany leadership during the rise of the Industrial Revolution, in 1879, Wesley Chapel's next pastor, Reverend J.L. Pitner (1877-80), struck a nativist, anti-immigrant theme against trade unions and the strikers, noting that many of the poorest laborers were recent immigrants: "We cannot consent for Europe to skim her slums and dash the scum onto our faces, without a protest."[90] By 1880, a growing proportion of New Albany's workforce consisted of younger, unskilled immigrants who earned far less than their skilled, native-born, or white coworkers. A divided labor force confronted the "industrial barony" of DePauw, who allied with the native-born and protestant Gilded Age elite to control the local political economy.[91]

In January 1880, one of the pioneers of Wesley Chapel, Mary Wicks Stoy, passed away. Her husband, Peter Stoy, had been one of the first Trustees and founders of Wesley Chapel. She was present at the dedication of the first Wesley Chapel Church and had been a member since 1822. Her obituary read:

> …a most faithful, consistent, and influential member for 57 years. She will be greatly missed from her loved Church where through more than a half a century her example spoke words of such winning eloquence and potential influence. She never missed the regular services of the Church when within her power to be present and took great delight urging others to live lives of devotion to Christ and the Church. By none will she be more sincerely mourned than her sisters and brothers at Wesley Chapel. Her funeral was held at Wesley Chapel and presided over by the Reverend J.L. Pitner.[92]

The 49th Indiana Methodist Conference was held in New Albany in September of that same year, as Joseph Shell Woods (1880-83) began shepherding the church. Wesley Chapel had 482 members, and the Sunday School program was in a "flourishing condition" at that time.[93] Reverend Woods, who also served as Pastor in 1872-74, was "strong and positive" and "able to adorn his sermons with the most delicate touches of imagery." As a person, he "had the faculty of making people feel that they could confide in and trust him implicitly."[94] He counseled and ministered to the famous New Albany steamboat builder, Captain Thomas Humphrey, during the last few months of the captain's life in 1881.[95] Later, Woods received an honorary doctorate from DePauw University.

It was during this era that the church periodically held a Love Feast. Members who were in good standing (meaning their regular contributions were in "good standing") were symbolically given a feast of "bread and water." This Love Feast was held consistently until 1900, when Reverend F. A. Steele was pastor.[96]

Woods was succeeded by Reverend Allen R. Julian (1883-85), a graduate of DePauw University who also practiced law in Bowling Green, Kentucky. Julian presided over the funeral of one of the founding members of Wesley, John Angell, in August 1885. He left New Albany at the end of 1885 to preach in Princeton, Indiana, and returned to serve for two years as

Presiding Elder (District Superintendent) on the New Albany circuit. He then sought "the frontier life," and moved to Nebraska to preach and work his ranch.⁹⁷

The railroad bridge across the Ohio River was completed in 1886, during the second year of Reverend Howard Willis (1885-90) term. By then, a divided working class made few demands of the city's political leaders, who were fearful of antagonizing DePauw.⁹⁸ New Albany was reflective of the era in the United States known as the Gilded Age, when tremendous industrial wealth was controlled by a small elite class.

Reverend Willis, a graduate of DePauw University who had served in the Civil War, was an "eloquent and feeling speaker."⁹⁹ He started a class for deaf mutes directed by the Reverend Philip J. Hasenstab, also a deaf mute.¹⁰⁰ It was under Pastor Willis that a new pipe organ was installed in the Church in 1887.¹⁰¹

Post Card circa 1890. New Albany Churches. Courtesy of Stuart B. Wrege Indiana History Room, New Albany Floyd County Public Library.

CHAPTER 4 • 45

In the late 1880s, the discovery of natural gas in east-central Indiana dramatically affected the glass industry in New Albany. It was a cheaper fuel and caused some of the glass industry to leave New Albany, while others went out of business due to competition from glass industries that used natural gas. Growing demand for lumber products resulted in tremendous growth for the veneer and plywood industries in the city by the turn of the century.

Reverend Emmons Rutledge Vest (1890-94), came to Wesley in 1890. That year the population of New Albany stood at 21,059, and people began to move outside the city center.[102] A graduate of and professor at DePauw University, Vest authored at least three books, including *Columbia's Tomorrow, Religion in Civilization,* and *Higher Citizenship*.[103] Peter Raymond Stoy, the son of founding members of Wesley, Peter and Mary Wicks Stoy, died in 1892 and Pastor Vest presided over his funeral.

Reverend Emmons R. Vest and his wife, Celestia[104]

Reverend Clippinger, a DePauw graduate, came to Wesley Chapel in 1894. On December 30, 1896, he performed the marriage of Charles Prosser, the science teacher at New Albany High School, and Zevelda Huckeby.[105] Prosser is considered the "father of vocational education" in the United States. The following year, Clippinger, whose father was also a Methodist minister, organized an "Old Person's Day" on June 13. He provided carriages for 16 elderly people who otherwise could not have made it to Church. Among these was 93-year old Elizabeth Brown Beeler, better known as "Mother Beeler," the first person to become a member of Wesley.[106] F.A. Steele replaced Clippinger n 1898 and served until the turn of the century. Wesley Chapel had been in existence for over 80 years, enduring and flourishing through war, depression, and revolution. Just as their traditional "Love Feast" came to an end at the dawn of 1900, the members of Wesley Chapel knew it was time to face forward and bravely look ahead to a new age.

Sailing into Headwinds:
The New Century, WWI, and the Roaring Twenties

Putting out to sea…we encountered strong headwinds that made it difficult to keep…on course…
Acts 27:4 (NLT)

By the late 1800s and early 1900s, the social gospel movement emerged as a response to the so-called sins of the industrial revolution and the Gilded Age including poverty, economic inequality, child labor, and unsafe working conditions. This movement merged with the Progressive Movement of the first two decades of the 20th century.

Of the eight individuals who served as pastors of Wesley Chapel during those twenty years, little is recorded about the tenure of the first three, John H. Ward (1900-02), J.B. Smith (1902-03), and H.H. Allen (1903-05), with the exception of Reverend Smith. He was known as a man of "unflinching integrity" who left after one year due to ill-health.[107]

In 1907, the Methodist Church was the first to adopt the Social Creed of the Churches, which called for the alleviation of Sunday working hours, the elimination of child labor, safer working conditions in factories, a living wage, and the provision of disability insurance for workers in factories. The Social Creed was placed in the Methodist Book of Discipline and has been revised over the years.[108]

With W.R. Plummer (1905-09) serving as pastor during this period, the Church raised $1000 for a new parsonage. In 1908 the members recorded they were "more than pleased with [Reverend Plummer's] strong sermons."[109] He left the following year to become the Rector of St. Paul's Protestant Episcopal Church in Louisville.[110]

Reverend Lawrence C. Jeffrey (1909-14) came to Wesley Chapel that year, and the following year there were plans to merge Main Street Methodist Church with Wesley Chapel, but the members of Main Street voted against the plan to abandon their building.[111] After several years of raising funds, the old parsonage, which had been used since 1851, was torn down, and a new parsonage was constructed on the same site on Lafayette Street in 1910.[112] Pastor Jeffrey played a key role in the New Albany District Epworth League, which focused on developing a Christ-centered character in young adults.[113]

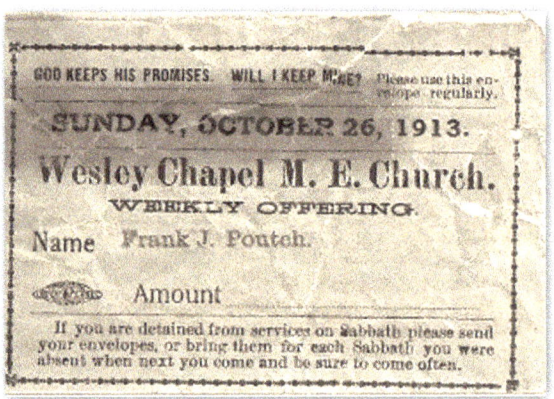

Offering Envelope from 1913.
Courtesy of Bill Amerson.

Woodrow Wilson, who was a student under social gospel leader and economist Richard Ely, was elected president in 1912 with the support of the progressive and the social gospel movements. On Sunday, October 19, 1913, during the centennial celebration of Wesley Chapel's New Albany location, all of the Methodist Churches held an "Old Time Singing Service" at Wesley. Testimonies and talks by lay members were part of the service, but it was noted that "when these became too lengthy, someone would break forth into singing, and the speaker was sung down."[114]

Program from the "Old time Singing" Service, October 19, 1913. Courtesy of Bill Amerson

The members of Wesley celebrated the "burning" of the last note on the parsonage in late 1913.[115] According to the Western Christian Advocate, Reverend Jeffrey had "the most successful year of his five years in this honored historic church" in 1914. [116] A new pipe organ was installed in the Church that year, and Wesley fielded its first baseball team that competed in a church league.[117] The Indiana Conference was held in New Albany, and the Wesley Chapel Choir provided the music.

On October 27 of the following year, the current pastor, Reverend O.C. Haley (1914-16), received additional comforts as the members of Wesley Chapel gave some household items and a new iron stove was put in the parsonage.[118] A steam heating plant was also installed in the church.[119]

The following year, there was a citywide "Go to Church" day on January 10 that was led by Wesley Chapel and Pastor Haley. The event was considered a "splendid success."[120] Later in life, Reverend Haley reminisced about his "men only" meetings with 200 to 300 in attendance. He remembered, "What a joy it was to preach in the W.C. [Wesley Chapel] auditorium" with "that majestic organ and splendid choir."[121]

Postcard from 1915. Methodist Episcopal Churches in New Albany. Courtesy of Stuart B. Wrege Indiana History Room, New Albany-Floyd County Public Library.

Later in 1916, as Woodrow Wilson campaigned for what would be his presidential re-election, Reverend W.G. Morgan (1916-18) began his term, placing him at Wesley Chapel's helm during the extremely difficult events that would follow. On March 23, 1917, a devastating tornado hit New

Albany, killing at least 45 people, destroying more than 300 homes, and leaving more than 2,500 people homeless. The church was not damaged, and the members helped in the clean-up of the damaged areas of the city. In June of that year, Wesley Chapel celebrated its Centennial Anniversary with a Love Feast, which had been a regular event at Wesley Chapel until 1900. Celebration meetings were held each night of the week from June 17-24.[122]

Hoosiers, especially Methodists, largely supported American neutrality during WWI until Germany began the practice of unrestricted submarine warfare in February of 1917. The United States declared war against Germany on April 6 of that year. To wage war, the federal government expanded dramatically, organized industrial production, obtained no-strike guarantees from the growing labor movement, and instituted a compulsory military draft. Economic opportunities for minorities and women increased, and many African-Americans began to migrate from the south to the industrial cites of the Midwest. Members of the Methodist Church, most supportive of the social gospel movement, believed that "saving the world for democracy was viewed as a Christian duty." Liberty bonds were sold in Methodist Churches and patriotic sermons were common.[123]

Young men, including African-Americans, were either drafted or volunteered to fight in Europe. Almost two million Americans had served in France by the end of the war, and 130,000 were Hoosiers. Some of these young men, such as Paul Seabrook, the great grandson of Daniel Seabrook, worshipped at Wesley Chapel. Reverend R.W. Fish (1918-20) was appointed to serve the church two months before the signing of the armistice that ended WWI on November 11, 1918.

After WWI, pent-up demand and spending created a period of inflation followed by a two-year recession. By 1922, the economy had begun to grow again, and America prospered until 1929. Much of this prosperity was based upon the business-government partnership that had been created during WWI. A consumer-oriented society developed as worker productivity and wages for labor increased. Yet, there was a downside to this prosperity. Businesses and both national and state governments opposed, often violently, unionization and the national labor movement. African-American migration to the industrial urban north, coupled with immigration from southern and eastern Europe, primarily Catholics, led to a nativist backlash. In response to the "immigration issue," the national government cut quotas from those regions in the mid-1920s. African-American demands for equal treatment led to the rise of the Ku Klux Klan once again, especially in the urban areas of Indiana. Yet, of all major cities in Indiana, New Albany had the smallest percentage of population associated with the Klan. This was due in part to the anti-Klan community leadership not only in New Albany but also in Louisville, Kentucky.[124]

New Albany prospered in the 1920s. With a population of 22,292 in 1920, it was the second largest city in the state and the world's largest producer of plywood and veneer. The garment industry, M. Fine and Sons and H.A. Seinsheimer Clothing Factory, began to provide employment to women who worked outside the home. The present-day New Albany High School was built in 1927. The following individuals served as Pastors from 1920 to 1928: James Wesley Turner (1920-23) and J.G. Sibson (1923-28). Pastor Turner, a graduate of Moore's College, came to Wesley in 1920. That year, there was a plan to close Wesley Chapel and unite with Centenary, but members voted against it. Wesley Chapel members remodeled classrooms from 1922 to 1926, redecorated the interior, placed new lights in the sanctuary, acquired new equipment, and tuck-pointed and painted the exterior of the building at a cost of $3,800.[125] The Church purchased the property to its east, razed the tenement houses, and built a two-story red brick structure for a new parsonage. Pastor Sibson and his family were the first to live in the new parsonage in 1927.

As Herbert D. Bassett (1928-33) began his extended pastoral term, no one could have predicted the economic and political upheavals that would occupy the world for nearly the next two decades, severely testing the members of Wesley Chapel and forcing them to rely upon their faith in God, perhaps more than at any time in their history.

Surviving Hurricanes: The Great Depression, the Flood of 1937, and WWII

God is our refuge and strength, always ready to help in times of trouble. So, we will not fear...
Psalm 46: 1-2 (NLT)

The Great Depression was perhaps the most important event in the history of the United States and the world in the 20th century. It dramatically altered the political, economic, and social landscapes of the United States, played a role in the rise of fascism in Europe and Asia, and ultimately led to WWII. By 1932, industrial output in the United States had declined by 50 percent since the stock market crash in October of 1929. Hundreds of banks had failed. The numbers of homeless people multiplied, and tent cities or shantytowns known as "Hoovervilles" appeared in every major city. Bread and soup lines became common. Unemployment in southern Indiana and New Albany was greater than 50 percent during the worst years of the depression, and as many as 99,000 Hoosiers came to work for the Works Progress Administration, which focused on building infrastructure in the state while providing jobs for people. They constructed more than 24,000 miles of roads, 3000 bridges, 361 state parks, and 78 schools.

Wesley Chapel faced membership problems during the depression, forcing the pastors to engage in deliberate outreach and membership-building programs and rely heavily upon the lay leadership. Reverend Bassett was pastor when the stock market crashed in 1929. As part of his outreach efforts, a church basketball team was organized, and it competed in the church league for the next two decades.[126] There was much talk of closing the church during the term of Pastor H.W. Baldridge (1933-36), but members, as they had done several times in the past, voted against it in early 1936.[127] Baldridge was remembered as being "tall, gray-haired, and impressive."[128]

Reverend Charles R. Query (1936-39), who almost always dressed in formal attire, arrived at Wesley in 1936 and immediately began an effort to build a new leadership group that was committed to keeping the church doors open.[129] Within a short time, he had to deal with a crisis, as torrential rains from January 9 to 23, 1937, raised the Ohio River to the highest levels ever recorded. The flood affected all of those along the Ohio River from Pittsburgh to Cairo, Illinois. More than a million people were left homeless. The river rose 60.8 feet, and most of New Albany was under 10 feet of water for three weeks. It is estimated that 40 percent of the population of the city had to be evacuated. Wesley Chapel suffered considerably. "The

Downtown New Albany during the 1937 Flood. Courtesy of Stuart B. Wrege Indiana History Room, New Albany-Floyd County Public Library.

water reached a stage of five feet on the first floor, inflicting serious loss on furniture and fixtures. Rehabilitation of the Sunday School rooms, the halls, and entire first floor of the parsonage was necessary."[130] Emma Oldham, a member at the time, indicated that the floodwater destroyed many church records, and "a lot of the [members'] morale went with them."[131] Mary M. Streepy Stoy, the third wife of Daniel B. Stoy (who was a son of Peter and Mary Wicks Stoy, one of the founding families of Wesley Chapel), died at the age of 94 on March 9, 1937, after having to leave her house in downtown New Albany to escape the flood. According to Pastor Query, 95 percent of the members of the Church had to leave their homes due to the high water.[132]

Wesley Chapel during the 1937 Flood. Courtesy of Stuart B. Wrege Indiana History Room, New Albany-Floyd County Public Library.

Many of the members wanted to close the church, but Pastor Query "held tenaciously to the idea that the church had a good future with younger leadership."[133] Wesley Chapel gradually recovered as the members began repairing and making improvements to the floodwater damage to the church and parsonage. Just as Pastor Query had predicted, young lay leadership played a primary role in saving the church. Wesley celebrated its 120th anniversary on June 4, 1937. Pastor Query delivered the sermon, "The Unfinished Task of the

Church," at the celebration. It was under Pastor Query that women, for the first time, served as stewards of the Church.[134] By the end of his term in 1939, the church budget was in excellent shape, and there was $2800 in the endowment fund.[135] Despite this, membership continued to be a significant concern for Wesley.

Reverend Lester N. Abel (1939-40), who had been an executive secretary at Taylor University, served one year at Wesley before becoming a Chaplain in the US Army.[136] The Women's Society of Christian Service, with 76 charter members, was created in September 1940 by merging the Women's Foreign Missionary Society and the Women's Home Missionary Society.[137] This new organization was the precursor to United Methodist Women, and was designed to increase and develop leadership and service opportunities for women. Stella Newhouse served as the first president, and Mrs. Harry Mann acted as secretary. Several improvements were made to the large Sunday School room during the pastorate of Hugh W. Glenn (1940-42), who often took members of the congregation fishing with him. Membership continued to be an issue, even as the first "junior" choir at Wesley was created in 1941.[138]

Between the two world wars, a "wave of pacifism" spread through much of the Methodist Church. The violence associated with modern warfare and the more than nine million deaths during WWI led to a disillusionment with war and caused many Methodists to question the role of the United States in the conflict. The Methodist Church publicly stated its opposition to a United States intervention into the war in Europe in 1939. Hoosier Methodists, like most Methodists across the country, were not in favor of American involvement in WWII until the Japanese attack on Pearl Harbor on December 7, 1941. Many had returned home from church and just finished lunch when news of the attack was heard over the radio. The attack led to a groundswell of support for the war effort among the Methodist laity. Shortly after Pearl Harbor, Pastor Glenn left the church to become a chaplain in the US Army during the war and he served in that capacity until 1951.[139] Reverend Carl Allinger, who left his previous church after the events of Pearl Harbor because his "views on the war were not acceptable to many of the members," was assigned to Wesley Chapel in 1942.[140]

Pastor Allinger and his wife, Emma, arrived at a critical time. Not only were young men from New Albany leaving for war, but also there was, again, much talk of closing the church. He wrote that:

> Market Street Church [Wesley Chapel] in New Albany was a "has been." At one time, it was the best church in that district, but when I moved there in 1942, they were about ready to close the door. They had a Board meeting to close the church. Seven were present and three voted to close with four voting to keep it open. They decided that seven was not a fair sample, so they called another meeting. Thirteen attended that meeting, and seven voted to keep it open and six opposed, so you can see that the church was hanging on a string.[141]

Reverend Carl Allinger and his wife Emma Courtesy of Jaclyn Heeke, granddaughter of the Allingers.

Pastor Allinger was successful in turning around Wesley Chapel by focusing on young people. He wrote that during his tenure, "there was no more talk of closing.... When I left, Wesley Chapel had the most active and best youth organization in the district."[142] He regularly attended sporting events at New Albany High School, and early in his pastorate, he organized the Methodist Youth Fellowship, which included those between the ages of twelve and twenty-three.[143]

During WWII, several young men from Wesley served in Europe and the Pacific. A few young men, including Darryl Grose, were killed. Life on the home front in New Albany was difficult. The Women's Society of Christian Service regularly sent cards to the service men on their birthdays and holidays.[144] With the government restructuring the economy to support the war effort, most goods were rationed, and many who lived in urban areas planted "victory gardens" to supplement their food needs. The daily war news dominated the radio, the theatres, and the newspapers, and the fear that loved ones would never return from the Pacific or Europe was always present. The war years took a toll on Pastor Allinger. He wrote that, "At the end of the fourth year, I had to leave. I don't know why, but I felt I couldn't take anymore."[145]

Reverend Chester L. Hughbanks served as pastor for five months in 1946 but left that fall for health reasons. It was under Pastor Hughbanks that a softball team was put together that played in the church league for many years.[146] Membership stood at 350 in 1946, as the world was soon to be transformed by another kind of war.[147]

The Old Ship Journeys through Favorable Winds: Post-WWII to the Mid-1960s

When times are good, be happy...
ECCLESIASTES 7:14

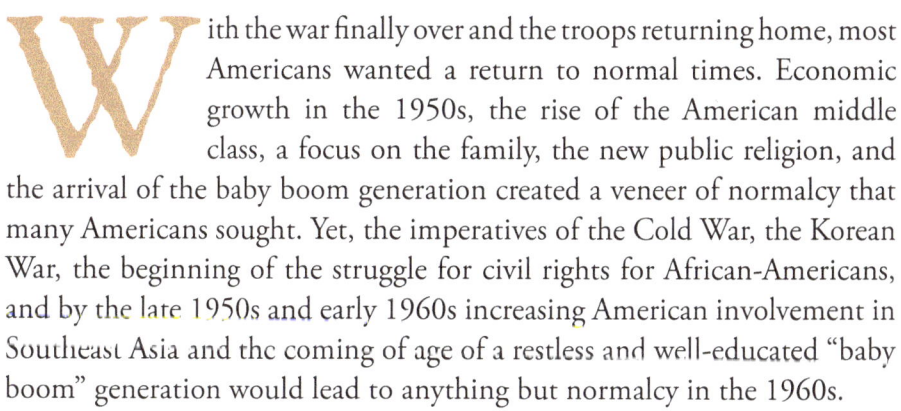

With the war finally over and the troops returning home, most Americans wanted a return to normal times. Economic growth in the 1950s, the rise of the American middle class, a focus on the family, the new public religion, and the arrival of the baby boom generation created a veneer of normalcy that many Americans sought. Yet, the imperatives of the Cold War, the Korean War, the beginning of the struggle for civil rights for African-Americans, and by the late 1950s and early 1960s increasing American involvement in Southeast Asia and the coming of age of a restless and well-educated "baby boom" generation would lead to anything but normalcy in the 1960s.

Church attendance in the country increased under the new public religion practiced by the Eisenhower administration. Church membership among Americans had increased from 43 to 49 percent between 1910 and 1940. The religious revival of the 1940s and 1950s, led by Christian libertarians such as James Fifield, Jr., had originally been organized by big business to counter the New Deal in the 1930s. It found a public voice in President Dwight Eisenhower and was used to counter the "godless communist threat" of the Soviet Union during the height of the Cold War. Church membership in the United States reached an all-time high of 67 percent by 1960.[148] This membership growth was also reflected in Wesley Chapel.

Reverend William Amos "WA" Amerson, a graduate of Texas Tech University, Asbury Theological Seminary, and Louisville Presbyterian Seminary, became Pastor of Wesley Chapel in November 1946. On that first Sunday, Pastor Amerson wrote, "There were 101 persons in church, mostly to observe and critique this new young preacher."[149] This was the largest crowd to attend Wesley in several years. Reverend Amerson began with a staff that included his wife, Virginia, and Stella Newhouse, who worked only three days a week. Deliberate outreach efforts into the community paid off as membership began to grow under Pastor Amerson, who had "never met a stranger."[150] The first coed Sunday School class of Wesley Chapel was the Christian Homebuilders, formed in 1947. This class, along with the Homemakers, provided much of the younger lay leadership.

Reverend W.A. Amerson, Pastor of Wesley Chapel 1946-56. Courtesy of Bill Amerson.

The church started a monthly newsletter in 1948 called The Wesley Whirl, which indicated on the front page that it was "the Church that Cares." This expression is still identified with the church today. The Wesley Whirl, initially edited by Marilyn Koehler and Glenda Garland, gave updates and activities concerning worship services, Sunday School, and a sports roundup. The newsletter and a church sports program were evidence of the intentional outreach program under Pastor Amerson.[151] Other outreach included the Mid-Week Reminder and the Chapel Keyhole, prepared by the Homebuilders class. Pastor Amerson and Virginia had a deep commitment to missions and were continually encouraging persons who were "called to ministry." They often sent gifts to missionaries or to persons preparing for the ministry.[152]

The sanctuary at Wesley Chapel while Reverend Amerson was Pastor, 1946-56. Courtesy of Bill Amerson.

The Church purchased robes for the choir for the first time in 1948, just in time for Palm Sunday on March 21.[153] After a short time, the sanctuary was redecorated. An educational unit was built for $30,000 in 1951. The unit was built with volunteer labor from church members, but it was made possible because of a donation from the estate of Mrs. Mamie Friend St. Onge, former member of Wesley Chapel and daughter of I.B. Friend.[154] The same year, the Mary Martha Circle was created, which empowered women to play greater leadership roles in the life of Wesley Chapel. Church membership reached 600 by 1953.[155]

Throughout January and early February of the next year, the Church celebrated its 137th Anniversary as well as its centennial celebration at that location. The celebration included the dedication of its new educational hall, the staging of a historical pageant, and a note-burning ceremony for all the loans associated with the property and its buildings. Reverend Chester A. McPheeters, a former youth at Wesley and the Pastor at the Metropolitan Methodist Church in Detroit, was the guest speaker. Reverend McPheeters commented later in a letter to Pastor Amerson that, "I think I have never seen Wesley in as good repair, and with such high morale."[156] On September 16, 1956, there were 610 people in attendance on the last Sunday that Pastor Amerson preached. Church membership had reached 689 by that time.[157]

Reverend Dahlgren L. Casey, who had been an Army Chaplain, and his wife, Aca, arrived at Wesley in September. He served as Pastor from September 23, 1956, until June 1959. The Indiana Annual Conference was held at Wesley in October 1956, with Bishop Richard Raines presiding.

Wesley Chapel with parsonage in the early 1960s. Courtesy of Stuart B. Wrege Indiana History Room, New Albany-Floyd County Public Library.

64 • SAIL ON OLD SHIP

Lynn Dennison, a former youth at Wesley, enrolled as a ministerial student at Asbury College that year and later became a Methodist Minister. Many others followed his example.[158]

Reverend Lloyd Shannon, a graduate of Asbury College and Asbury Seminary, became Pastor in the summer of 1959. He arrived with his wife, Virginia, and their five daughters. Virginia reminisced about life at Wesley Chapel:

> There used to be a saloon down the street, and on Friday nights, Lloyd would find drunks passed out on the lawn of the Church. He would bring them into the basement of the church and let them sleep it off. You never knew who you would find in that old basement on Saturday mornings.[159]

Wesley Chapel needed much work by 1959. Remodeling and repairs were going to be very expensive. In September, Wesley Chapel purchased the Carney property at 2212 State Street for a new parsonage, along with two acres of ground. The old parsonage, next to the Church, was converted to a youth center with several classrooms. Pastor Shannon and Virginia held an open house at the new parsonage in December 1959.

Wesley Chapel float during the Sesquicentennial of the city of New Albany in October 1963. Courtesy of Stuart B. Wrege Indiana History Room, New Albany-Floyd County Public Library.

On May 11, 1960, the Trustees, consisting of Ewell Wolfe, Calvin Appelhaus, Harold Bierod, Fred Canter, Orville Donan, Millard Kendall, Lafayette LaDuke, Clarence Roederer, and Gordon Sadler, purchased an additional acre of ground adjacent to the recently acquired property on State Street. The congregation reluctantly voted for relocation on March 5, 1961, believing that the youth could better be served in a new building and location. While some members were fearful that the church could not win any new members in an area that was considered a "Catholic community," the Indiana Methodist Conference supported the move, believing that it needed a strong presence in that part of the city.[160] The Old Ship was put up for sale on November 25 of that year and sold to the local newspaper, the New Albany Tribune, on June 2, 1963, for $50,000.[161]

Over the course of the next year, a significant revival was led by the Reverend Bill Arnett which brought many people to Christ, even some who had been with Wesley Chapel for many years. The final service at the Old Ship was held on June 7, 1964, and the next month the 110-year-old structure was razed to make way for a new building for the city newspaper.[162] Five windows from the church, originally dedicated to the Stoy and Beeler families, were purchased by the Stoy family. The congregation met at the Masonic Lodge until the new church building was ready. Ground was broken for the new Wesley Chapel on the State Street property on a windy and cool but sunny day on January 26, 1964, at 2:30 p.m. More than 175 members attended, as Lay Leader Bill Schuppert spoke:

> For it was some 110 years ago, on a Sunday afternoon in 1854, that a loyal group of Christians gathered together on a lot at West 2nd and Market Streets to take part in a very significant ceremony, that of breaking ground for their new Wesley Chapel Church. The meeting of those Christians there that day had far reaching effects on many lives, even up to this day....For I am sure that all of us love that old church, and it is with the same reluctance with which they left their old church that we leave ours.
>
> But now the time is at hand for us to move forward. We are on the threshold in our church history. Now we stand, as they stood a century ago. And with the same faith, the same courage, sacrifice,

and love, we break this ground and dedicate this hallowed spot to God and His Work, to be a Lighthouse to this community…[163]

Groundbreaking on State Street, January 26, 1964. Reverend Lloyd Shannon is in the center of the picture. Courtesy of Wesley Chapel United Methodist Church.

Stanley Marcum of Louisville designed the new church building, and a contract was signed with Earle Embry and Son, General Contractors of New Albany, to build it. Some members noted that it resembled an inverted ship's hull. It included 18 classrooms in the educational wing designed to focus on the youth, the future of the church. The first services were held on October 18, and Pastor Shannon remarked, "Wesley Chapel, the Old Ship, sails on in majestic splendor." It was consecrated on January 24, 1965, with Bishop Richard Raines preaching and conducting the ceremony. The Memorial Chapel, below the new sanctuary, contained some items from the old church, including the pulpit, two large carved chairs, the marble-topped communion table, a 100-year-old communion service, the communion rail, the baptismal front, nine of the old pews, the perpetual light, and a large 77-year-old Bible donated in 1937 by one of the members of the congregation, Mrs. Vina Bruder. The Bible was bought by her late husband, Herbert Bruder, at age 14 and presented to his mother.[164]

Wesley Chapel in the mid-1960s. Courtesy of Wesley Chapel United Methodist Church.

Five members of Wesley Chapel were ordained as ministers at the annual Methodist Conference in June of that year. They were the Reverend Robert Eve (a graduate of the Ohio Methodist Theological Seminary), the Reverend Arlington S. "Joe" Hook, the Reverend Lynn Denison (a graduate of Asbury Theological Seminary), the Reverend Jerry Dehn, and the Reverend Alvin L. Mattox.

From the very beginning, women have always played major roles in the life of Wesley Chapel. The Women's Society for Christian Service, the precursor to United Methodist Women, consisted of three "circles," or groups of women, at Wesley. By 1965, the Mary Martha Circle and the Virginia Ruth Circle were already encouraging and providing leadership and service opportunities for women. The third group, the Rebekah Circle, was formed on January 17, 1966, with 14 members at its first meeting. Colleen Shannon LaDuke was elected as the first chairperson.[165] One of the most exemplary female leaders, Miss Stella Newhouse, passed away on January 4, 1966. Her life was remembered by all and is illustrated in her own testimony: "I firmly believe that stewardship is a way of life. I do not propose to enjoy the fruits of Christianity and neglect to cultivate the roots."[166] Membership at Wesley Chapel stood at 545 as of May 1, 1966.[167]

Shifting Winds and Full Sail Ahead: The Mid-1960s to 1998

In everything he did he had great success, because the Lord was with him.
1 Samuel 18:14

The issue of segregation in the 1950s split the Methodist Church along geographic and generational lines. Many young people in the Methodist Church were the first to support the end of "Jim Crow" and often faced opposition from the older generations within the church. Methodist churches in the south were more likely to support segregation than those in the north. While the Church tried to protect Methodist ministers in the south who preached against segregation, it was a difficult time for these individuals. Some moved to states in the north, including Indiana. Future Wesley Chapel minister, the Reverend Huie Holloway from Georgia, whose family was in the peanut industry, was one such minister.[168]

The civil rights movement was at its height in the mid-1960s. By that time, American involvement in Southeast Asia had increased dramatically, and by 1968, more than a half a million troops were in Vietnam. Early that year, the Tet Offensive turned the American people against the war effort and energized anti-war demonstrations on college campuses and in major cities. The Methodist General Conference in 1968 and 1970 openly urged the US government to withdraw troops from Vietnam, and in 1972, it condemned the American intervention in Vietnam as a "crime against humanity."[169] The 1960s counterculture movement and the struggle for women's rights gained support. At the same time, the country began to experience a decline in church attendance and membership, which would last until the 1980s. Despite the national trend, attendance and membership at Wesley Chapel remained consistent and strong.

Reverend Richard D. Armstrong. Courtesy of Bill Amerson.

Reverend Richard "Dick" Armstrong, a graduate of Asbury College, his wife, Jean, and their two children came to Wesley Chapel in June 1966. Pastor Armstrong, a "friend to all," was a "people person" and known for his "inspiring" sermons and willingness to minister to the sick and the elderly during the week.[170] Wesley celebrated its sesquicentennial with a celebration throughout October and November of 1967. Events included several fellowship opportunities, a historical pageant, talks by Bishop Richard Raines and former Pastors Carl Allinger, Lloyd Shannon, and W.A. Amerson, and a concert by the Korean Orphans Choir. By this time, membership began to reflect more than the local community of New Albany. Wesley Chapel was now a regional church, with membership from several surrounding counties in Indiana and Louisville.

The Lamplighters Sunday School class remodeled the offices in the church with money from their annual Spook Run in October 1971. Reverend Armstrong was involved in a rather humorous event in the offices of the Floyd County Alcoholic Beverage Board. In 1973, Taylor Drug Store, located in the New Albany Plaza 178 feet from Wesley Chapel, attempted to obtain a liquor license from the Floyd County Alcoholic Beverage Board. Despite the fact that the law required a distance of at least 200 feet between it and Wesley Chapel, the lawyers for Taylor Drug Store appealed to Pastor Armstrong to write a letter in support of the liquor license grant. This was probably the first time in history that a minister of a church had been asked to take such a position. Pastor Armstrong, backed by a crowd of women from the church, told the members of the board, "I cannot write such a letter." The lawyers for the drug company chuckled and said, "By the way, come in and see us for your drugs."[171]

The Church and the parsonage debts were paid off in September 1973. Pastor Armstrong continued to focus on evangelism and mission outreach. Wesley saw an increase in youth involvement, and its youth programs flourished.[172] A Lay Witness Weekend in 1974 led to a major spiritual renewal in which many people gave their lives or recommitted their lives to Christ. Several other revivals led to a significant spiritual growth among the laity, especially the youth. By 1975, the Salvation Army was regularly recognizing the members of Wesley Chapel for their volunteer efforts, as it still does today.

In June 1977, Reverend Milton "Huie" Holloway, a graduate of Auburn University and the Candler School of Theology at Emory University, was assigned to replace the very popular Pastor Armstrong. The Church continued to grow, and new Sunday School classes were started during the pastorate of Reverend Holloway, whose wife, Bonnie, was a nurse and not the typical "pastor's wife." She was reflective of both the aspiration of and increasing requisite for the wife to work outside the home in America. Many young families and couples, part of the baby-boom generation, found their way into Wesley Chapel's fellowship, including the newly created Contemporary Christian and Koinonia Sunday School

Reverend Huie Holloway. Courtesy of Bill Amerson.

classes. Members of these classes quickly moved into lay leadership positions. Pastor Holloway presided over the funeral of former pastor, the Reverend Lloyd Shannon, in 1981. With the surprising departure of Reverend Holloway in November, Reverend Lloyd Sawyer, with his wife, Dorothy, provided interim leadership until the conference assigned the Reverend John Thrasher to Wesley on January 15, 1982. Membership at Wesley stood at 532 at that time.

Reverend John Thrasher. Courtesy of Wilma Thrasher

The election of Ronald Reagan as President in 1980 ushered in a period in which the "Christian Right" began to exercise power in the Republican Party over social issues. The decline in national church membership and attendance rates since the mid-1960s was halted during the 1980s. The pastorate of John Thrasher, a graduate of Indiana State University and the Christian Theological Seminary, was an exciting period of growth and outreach. Pastor Thrasher, an avid sportsman who had a down-home, story-telling style of preaching, believed that the key to success is "to equip people to do ministry not only on the [church] campus, but also at work, at school, in their social lives, and other areas outside the Church."[173] He expected members to "walk the talk and get involved."[174]

Support for foreign missionaries increased under Pastor Thrasher and included those in Kenya, Haiti, Liberia, South Korea, Brazil, Honduras, and Zaire. The church began having a mission conference, which raised more than $50,000 annually.[175] For several years, the congregation had supported the Wings of Morning missionary family (Kenneth and Lorraine Enright) in Zaire. News of the crash of the only plane that the Enrights had for their work reached Wesley Chapel in June 1985. In response, "Jim Ingram captured a vision of great ministry. He walked to the Chancel Choir area and challenged the congregation to raise the necessary funds to replace the plane."[176] The congregation raised the $27,000 needed to replace the airplane and presented the Enright family with a check at a service at Wesley on September 22 of that same year.

Wings of Morning Fundraiser at Wesley Chapel, June-September 1985. Courtesy of Wesley Chapel United Methodist Church.

Pastor Thrasher decided that Wednesday evenings should consist of more than prayer meetings. New activities that focused on spiritual growth, such as Bible study groups and fellowship opportunities, were added. There was an increase in the number of members who came regularly to these Wednesday activities. Many of the senior members began serving as counselors and mentors to the youth and the new members. As the church continued to grow, an additional worship service was added to Sunday morning, and a Sunday evening service continued to meet the needs of the membership. Reverend Amerson returned to Wesley in 1984 on his retirement and served as the assistant pastor, with special emphasis on visitation and evangelism.

On December 2, 1984, the church celebrated the bicentennial of Methodism with a musical play, Visions of Wesley, written by member Mrs. Linda Hersman and Reverend Amerson. In addition to the Chancel Choir, more than 100 members of the church participated in the play.[177] The Keeper of the Cane program, which recognizes the oldest member of the congregation, started in October 1986. Reverend Amerson, at the request of Pastor Thrasher, created the Whosoever Will Sunday School class in 1991, which now is made up of some of the most senior members of Wesley Chapel. To honor its veterans, Wesley began a tradition in which members who had served in the armed forces were recognized on Sunday once a year. The tradition included the reading of the iconic poem, "In Flanders Fields," by Warren Slider, a WWII veteran. This is still done today, with Ed Snelling now reading "In Flanders Fields."

A Long-Range Planning Committee, chaired by Steve Latimer, was formed in August 1988 to make plans as Wesley approached a new decade and century. A building committee was formed, and the Dale property adjacent to the north was purchased in 1989. The church also purchased a house at 1212 Lexington Drive in New Albany to serve as the new parsonage. In the fall, a financial campaign successfully raised over $700,000 as a part of "Sharing the Vision" program. A Family Life Center was completed in January 1991, which included classrooms, a kitchen, and a large, multipurpose room.

Despite the beginning of a national decline in church attendance and membership in the early 1990s that continues today, membership at Wesley reached 823 people by 1992. It celebrated its 175th anniversary on April 28 and received 50 new members into the church that day.[178] The church created the Wesley Center in 1997 in the old Golden Corral building on the property adjacent to the parking lot. Members renovated the building, which was primarily used to support the growing youth program. While attendance at Sunday School averaged almost 600 people and the three morning services reached 1000 people in 1997, Pastor Thrasher was very good at making the church feel small, friendly, and inviting to its visitors and members.[179] He knew everyone by his or her first name. He and his wife, Wilma, were loved and cherished by all. Yet, the members of Wesley Chapel would soon be faced with a difficult decision and a transition period, which would test them and then lead them to a "leap of faith."

A Leap of Faith: Charting a New Course and Setting Sail Again

Commit your work to the Lord, and your plans will be established.
PROVERBS 16:3

Wesley Chapel had experienced more than a half a century of successful outreach and growth. It had benefitted from some of the best pastors in its history and a congregation who fully believed in and actively pursued its mission. However, the very popular Pastor Thrasher was leaving at the end of 1997, and he would prove to be a difficult act to follow. Reverends Mark and Rebecca "Becky" Suter, both graduates of Eastern Kentucky University and Asbury Theological Seminary, came to Wesley Chapel as co-pastors in 1998. They brought with them their two daughters and a dramatic change in the pulpit. Both used a more academic style in their sermons, which contrasted sharply with Reverend Thrasher's down-home, country sermons. Some in the congregation were not ready for a female pastor, and others wanted Pastor Becky to act as a pastor's wife rather than a co-pastor.

At the same time, the members faced a very difficult decision. The church structure needed significant repairs, and membership growth required an expansion of the facilities. However, an expansion would require more land than was available at the current site. The alternative was to seek a new location for Wesley Chapel. The Long-Range Planning Committee recommended that the congregation no longer pursue plans to expand facilities at the current location and begin a process leading to relocation. The committee recommended that a Building Committee be selected to search for land for a new church facility, that plans be developed for a new capital campaign, and that architectural services be secured. To the dismay of the church leadership, the membership rejected the recommendation on June 26, 1999. Another controversy arose over the music in the church. While music selection arouses some controversy in almost all churches, this time several high-profile choir members chose to leave Wesley. Yet, God was at work because this group helped to create yet another church in New Albany, the New Beginnings Community Church.

The Suters emphasized the need for people to experience a growing, personal relationship with God through Jesus Christ. Under their leadership, missionary giving reached $80,000 per year, with funding to Zambia, Mexico, Guatemala, Honduras, Congo, Kenya, India, Uganda, Liberia, Sierra Leone, Ecuador, and Taiwan. The Helping Hands Ministry, led by Russ Denison, provided more than $30,000 per year to those who needed money for rent, food, utility bills, or gasoline.[180] Members took regular, short-term mission trips to St. Johns Island, South Carolina, and El Sembrador in Honduras. The Red Cross regularly used the facilities of Wesley for its blood drives, and the church maintained its strong relationship with the Salvation Army. Lay members continued their long history of hospital visitations.

On August 27, 2000, Co-Pastor Mark Suter announced that he and his wife, Co-Pastor Becky, were being reassigned to the First United Methodist Church of Martinsville. Reverend Donald "Don" R. Smith, a graduate of Hanover College and United Theological Seminary, his wife, Jane, and their family arrived that fall. Pastor Smith, who had a plainspoken style of preaching, taught that people need a relationship with God. He noted, "People need to realize that they are on a big search for something to fill up their lives, and everything they have found continues to leave a big hole until they fill it with a relationship with God."[181] He preached that it was this ongoing relationship with God that would lead to "faith in action."

The horrific events of September 11, 2001, occurred during the pastorate of Reverend Smith. The United Methodist Council of Bishops immediately issued a statement indicating that it believed that military action would not end terrorism. America's subsequent interventions in Afghanistan later that year, and especially in Iraq in 2003, illustrated the historic ambiguity of Methodists concerning issues of war and peace. The Church has always viewed war as incompatible with the teachings of Christ. While it officially opposes preemptive wars, it has supported defensive wars.

Yet, historically, the Methodist laity has always responded with support when America has gone to war, whether it was defensive or preemptive. As early as May 2002, the Methodist Council of Bishops and the General Board on Church and Society were supportive of America's right to self-defense but were publicly opposed to a preemptive intervention into Iraq. This opposition was publicly stated again when America invaded in March 2003. Yet, an overwhelming majority of churchgoing Americans, including Methodists, supported the preemptive intervention. In November 2005, more than half of the retired and active Bishops signed a letter condemning the "unjust and immoral invasion and occupation of Iraq." Other leaders in the Church, more reflective of the laity, expressed their opposition to the statements of the Bishops in media outlets such as the *Good News Magazine*.[182] This ambiguity was evident at Wesley Chapel in the muted controversy over the overt nationalism practiced during its Independence Day celebrations for several years after September 11, 2001.

Wesley Chapel continued its many successful outreach programs and developed new ones under the senior leadership of Pastor Smith. A very popular Gospel Night was held on November 3, 2002, when the choirs of Bethel AME Church, the Jones Memorial AME Church, and Wesley Chapel combined with the Mike Speck Trio. At its annual revival on September 19, 2004, Wesley invited several of its former members who had been called into the ministry to speak. These included John Abbott, Scott Engebretson, John Kesel, and Scott Wilson. A "50 Days of Love" campaign started later that month. A tutoring service was developed to help elementary, middle, and senior high school students. A Sunday School class was created specifically to address the needs of college students. Members took several short-term mission trips to Guatemala to help Steve and Pam Knight English, former members of Wesley, at La Senda, a home and school they had founded in 2001 for abused, abandoned, and orphaned children. A prayer blanket ministry was started. More than 200 members of Wesley carried out their "faith in action" by volunteering at the Silver Heights Camp and Retreat Center, the oldest "Bible camp" in the state.

Pastor Smith's wife, Jane, who was extremely popular and loved by all in the congregation for her endearing Mother's Day programs, passed away on December 3, 2009, after a prolonged struggle with cancer. Pastor Smith was unable to provide strong leadership on a day-to-day basis during her struggle. The lay leadership once again, as it had done many times in its history, stepped up and led Wesley to chart a new course.

Wesley Chapel as it appeared on State Street. Courtesy of Wilma Thrasher.

Developers, who saw the State Street property as valuable for retail space, approached the church in 2006-07. The members and lay leadership revisited the 1999 decision not to relocate. Dave Hussung and Shannon

Staten became co-chairs of a new Building Committee. Members included Bill Amerson, Amy Atkinson, Joe Brown, Russell Denison, Jim Ingram, Dan Johnson, Mike Miller, Becky Perkins, Rich Plass, Dennis Shireman, Tim Underwood, Paula Walker, Daryll Walters, and John Watkins. After an exhaustive, 18-month search for a suitable tract of land for a new church, the committee recommended that Wesley Chapel purchase 22 acres of land at the intersection of I-64 and Highway 150, develop an entry to the land from Highway 150, sell its State Street property, begin a capital campaign, and build a new church on the new property. The members of Wesley took a "leap of faith" and voted to support the recommendations of the committee on August 12, 2007. The new land was purchased, and the architectural firm of Akers and Associates was hired to design the new church building. John Hartstern and Dennis and Kara Reasoner led a Capital Campaign that began in 2008. By that time, there had been four failed attempts to sell the State Street property. The "Great Recession," which started in 2008, did not help as Wesley continued to seek a buyer for its property for the next three years. There was genuine concern that the value of the church property would plummet and adversely affect the ability to build on the new land.

Pastor Smith retired in late 2009, and Reverend Stephen "Steve" R. Seitz, a graduate of Oakland City University and United Theological Seminary, replaced him as interim Pastor. Pastor Seitz and his wife, Barb, provided stable leadership until the Reverend Richard Anthony "Tony" Alstott and his wife, Rhonda, and their five children came to Wesley Chapel in July 2010. Pastor Alstott, who grew up in the area and was a graduate of Indiana University Southeast and Southern Baptist Theological Seminary, worked with an active lay leadership that charted a course that led Wesley Chapel to play an even greater role in the local communities and to become a truly regional church. He stated, "Wherever God has sent me, my calling has been to share the love of Jesus and to reach into the community. And now, I get to reach into the community that helped shape me."[183]

A symbolic groundbreaking was held on the new property on Sunday, November 21, 2010, with more than 200 people participating. Bill Schuppert, who at that time had been a member of Wesley for 65 years and had spoken at the groundbreaking of the State Street church, stated, "I hate to see us leave New Albany for Floyds Knobs, but if that's where the Lord wants us to be, that's where we'll be."[184] A week later, the members took another "leap of faith" and said good-bye to the State Street property and church facilities. They gathered for one last picture in front of the building that had been used for 46 years and sang "Victory in Jesus" and "How Can I Keep from Singing." They opened the time capsule that had been buried when the church opened in 1964 and recited the poem, "The Old Ship," which had been identified with Wesley Chapel from its beginning.

Groundbreaking at the 150-Campus, November 21, 2010.
Shannon Staten (co-chair Building Committee), Steve Nash (Crossroads Construction), Reverend Stephen Seitz (former Pastor at Wesley Chapel in 2010), Pastor Tony Alstott, Reverend Don Smith (former Pastor at Wesley Chapel 2000-09), and Dave Hussung (co-chair Building Committee). Courtesy of Wesley Chapel United Methodist Church.

The members met at Christian Academy of Indiana the first Sunday in December. It was a temporary home for the next two years. The members began what Pastor Alstott called "tent camping," just as the Israelites had done in the desert for 40 years. Each Sunday, everything had to be set up and then taken down after the service in the school auditorium. While Wesley had a long history of serving its community, it was during this period that, according to Director of Worship, Tammy Ivey, "Our mindset became even more outward focused." Reverend Alstott preached that "In order to serve the community, you have to be in the community." Members continued the Helping Hands and Choices for Women Resource Center ministries. They continued their longtime and close association and work with the Salvation Army. They continued to provide tutoring services to elementary, middle, and senior high school students and established a partnership with the students at both Grant Line Elementary and Christian Academy. The ongoing Blessings in a Backpack campaign provided needy elementary school children food to take home during the school year. One of the new ministries was the Exit Zero Homeless Ministry. Teams of volunteers led by Bill Amerson helped with cleanup after tornadoes ravaged the Henryville and Borden areas in 2012.

The church then developed a multi-campus outreach. Dennis Alstott, Pastor of Grant Line United Methodist Church and father of Tony Alstott, was approached by his congregation to form a relationship with Wesley Chapel. Grant Line United Methodist Church voted to transfer the property to Wesley Chapel "for the glory of God" in December 2012, and it became a second campus of Wesley Chapel the following month. Several of the members of Grant Line United Methodist Church joined the Wesley Chapel congregation. As the congregation continued ministry from Christian Academy of Indiana, Grant Line United Methodist Church, and the temporary office space on Grant Line Road, its new campus at Highway 150 and I-64 began to take shape.

The members took yet another "leap of faith" in 2011 and negotiated a deal with the local banks to go ahead and build on the new property before the State Street property was sold. Your Community Bank and Wesley Chapel agreed to a three-million-dollar line of credit to assist in the construction. Members held several prayer walks on the new property that spring. In July 2011, Crossroads Construction began to build the nearly 48,000 square feet building that would become the fifth home of Wesley Chapel. Over the next few months while the bulldozers shaped the land, the leadership team began to negotiate with a new buyer of the State Street property. First Savings Bank purchased the State Street property in December 2011. The new owners named the old property Wesley Commons in a fitting tribute to Wesley Chapel's long presence on State Street.

The foundation for the new church at I-64 and Highway 150 was poured during the winter, and the steel frame arrived and began to be erected in February 2012. The concrete was poured for the stage area in March. Members contributed prayer and scripture rocks to be used for the stage foundation. The Wesley Chapel family was able to worship twice in the summer while the building was under construction. Pastor Alstott gave the message "So That," and an inspired congregation wrote the words "Glory to God" on the stage area. Another invitation was to write the names of people who were not Christian and commit to praying that they would become disciples of Jesus Christ. The steeple arrived in September. The evening of its arrival, several gathered to dedicate it to God's glory. Many wrote scripture verses on the inside of the steeple. The next day, the steeple was mounted on top of the building. On the very top of the cross of the steeple are the words, "Glory to God."

Placing the Steeple on Top of the Church, September 2012. Courtesy of Wesley Chapel United Methodist Church.

On February 3, 2013, Pastor Alstott opened the first worship service at the magnificent $8.2 million, 22-acre campus with Psalm 122:1: "I was glad when they said to me, 'Let us go into the house of the Lord.'" Alstott continued, "Upon this confession, the church of Jesus Christ is built, and upon this confession, the Wesley Chapel United Methodist Church is built." Worship attendance reached 600 that day. The message for the following week's service was "Leap of Faith." Rochelle Bishop took a "leap of faith" and became the first person at the Highway 150 Campus to come make a public profession of faith, while Derek Deacon took a "leap of faith" by asking Chandler Shaffer to marry him.

On March 24, 2013, Bishop Michael Coyner, District Superintendent Charlie Wilfong, Building Committee Co-Chairs Dave Hussung and Shannon Staten, and Highway 150 Campus Facilities Trustee Jeff Ganote dedicated the new church to the glory of God for the dual purposes of strengthening the faith of disciples and making disciples of Jesus Christ to transform the world. The church received 29 new members that day. During the remainder of the year, Wesley Chapel experienced what Pastor Alstott described as a Pentecost: "He added to their number daily."

Wesley Chapel United Methodist Church, the 150-Campus. Photo courtesy of Wesley Chapel United Methodist Church.

The move to the new location brought with it a change in the Sunday morning services, in particular a change in music. The Indiana Conference Fruitful Congregation Team evaluated the ministries at Wesley Chapel when it was meeting at Christian Academy of Indiana and presented a report to the congregation in January 2012. The report focused on both the strengths and areas of concern for the church and made some recommendations for the future. After a month of discussion and prayer by the congregation, it voted overwhelmingly to accept the recommendations as a blueprint for the future ministry of the church. The primary concern addressed in the report was that Wesley Chapel was an aging congregation and that it was imperative to begin to attract younger families and members. The report indicated that the current worship style was not attracting young people. Wesley had been offering a blended service since the 1990s. It included a choir that sang traditional hymns and some early and late 20th century music accompanied by a piano. According to the consultation report:

> Currently, the Sunday morning worship experiences are not reaching the desired audience of people ages 47 and under. This is due to a lack of clarity about the target audience and an understanding of the music and technology needed to reach this audience.

The leadership team made a decision to add a modern service consisting of praise music with a live band on Sunday evening at the Grant Line Campus. Attendance at this service quickly averaged 80 young people. When the members moved to the new 150 campus, one traditional and two modern worship services replaced the blended services on Sunday morning. This upset some members of the choir and the congregation. Some longtime members left Wesley Chapel over the next two years because they did not agree with the music changes, although a handful left for doctrinal issues that the Methodist Church was facing. Despite this, Wesley Chapel continued to grow under the new music format and began to attract younger families. As these younger families joined the church, the children's department grew beyond its initial capacity. By 2016, the children's department was taking care of an average of 60 children during worship. Attendance at Sunday morning services reached an average of 467 people, of whom many had only known Wesley Chapel at the 150 campus.[185]

The Indiana Conference Fruitful Congregation Team raised another concern in 2012. Despite the fact that the congregation fully embraced the mission to "make disciples," it was concerned about how the mission was being managed. The report indicated that there was no "clear discipleship pathway." Church leadership and members responded by initially defining the type of disciples its members should aspire to be. Paul wrote in Ephesians 3:17-18 that disciples are to be rooted and established in the love of Christ. Peter wrote in 2 Peter 3:18 that disciples are to grow in the grace and knowledge of Christ. The church developed a vision statement which asked its members to aspire to be "rooted in Christ and growing in grace." The church leadership developed "A Discipleship Pathway," which tracks how seekers become believers, believers become followers, and followers become ambassadors. Sermons, Bible studies, and faith-development life groups began to create curricula to address the needs of members on this discipleship pathway.

Wesley Chapel continues to welcome people from the entire Kentuckiana region in a friendly, warm, and inviting manner. Its Sunday services are full of young families. The Sunday School program maintains its tradition of excellence in teaching His truth and wisdom. "Wesley Wednesdays" continues to provide Christian fellowship and Bible study to its members, just as it has for so many years. The church's annual Easter Egg Hunt and Vacation Bible School continue to attract youth from the region. The members reach deep into the local communities with a variety of programs to do God's work under Pastor Alstott's exemplary leadership. Toward the end of 2016, the church leadership decided it was best to sell its Grant Line campus, and consistent with the history of Wesley Chapel, it came as no surprise that the new owners have started another church at that location.

Pastor Tony Alstott illustrating God's wisdom. Courtesy of Jim Ingram.

Wesley Chapel is proud of the long history of its members being called into the ministry and service to God. A brief list of some of the individuals includes Reverend Garry Abbott, Reverend John Abbott, Tony Benson, Reverend Jerry Dehn, Reverend Lynn Denison, Reverend Scott Engebretson, Ms. Pamela English, Reverend Chris Gadlage, Reverend David Hood, Reverend Joe Hook, Reverend John Kessel, Reverend Alvin Mattox, Reverend Ken Morgan, Reverend Kathryn Muhlbaier, Dennis Shireman, Dennis Tacket, Mr. Peter Williams, and the Reverend Scott Wilson. It is proud of the fact that at key times in its history, the laity, both men and women, has stepped up to provide necessary leadership and action. It is proud of its history of women who have served in leadership roles and as models of strength measured by their profound and visible faith. It is proud of its long line of highly educated ministers who have served with distinction as Captains of the "Old Ship."

Finally, as the "Old Ship" celebrates its Bicentennial on June 20, 2017, it is most important to note that its running lights are still bright and clear to all who seek Him and His grace. The members of Wesley Chapel are witnesses to its vision "being rooted in Christ and growing in grace," and they faithfully continue to carry on the mission "to make disciples of Jesus Christ to transform the world," just as they have done for the past 200 years.

Sail on "Old Ship,"
nor fear the gales,
Our hopes and prayers
will fill thy sails,
Until thy sails
at last are furled
In a new and ransomed world.

Ministers of Wesley Chapel

From 1817 to 1838, the Pastors of Wesley Chapel included Peter Cartwright, W. H. Goode, George Locke, Samuel Lowe, William McReynolds, William Shanks, John Shrader, John Strange, James Thompson, Calvin W. Ruter, and Allen Wiley.

1838-40 – John C. Smith

1840-42 – W.V. Daniel and Silas Rawson

1842-43 – George C. Beeks

1843-45 – Enoch G. Woods

1845-47 – Fernandez C. Holliday

1847-49 – James Hill

1849-50 – W.C. Smith

1850-52 – Hiram Gilmore

1852-54 – James H. Noble

1854-56 – J.Y. McKee

1856-57 – Benjamin F. Crary

1857-58 – Samuel Reed

1858-60 – S.B. Sutton

1860-62 – John M. Green

1862-64 – Hayden Hayes

1864-67 – James H. Noble

1867-70 – William McKendree Hester

1870-71 – Stephen Bowers

1871-72 – Aaron Turner

1872-74 – Joseph S. Woods

1874-77 – W.H. Grim

1877-80 – J.L. Pitner

1880-83 – Joseph S. Woods

1883-85 – Allen R. Julian

1885-90 – Tilghman Howard Willis

1890-94 – Emmons Rutledge Vest

1894-98 – H.C. Clilppinger

1898-1900 – F.A. Steele

1900-02 – John H. Ward

1902-03 – J.B. Smith

1903-05 – H.H. Allen

1905-09 – W.R. Plummer

1909-14 – L.C. Jeffrey

1914-16 – O.C. Haley

1916-18 – W.G. Morgan

1918-20 – R.W. Fish

1920-23 – James Wesley Turner

1923-28 – J.G. Sibson

1928-33 – Herbert D. Bassett

1933-36 – H.W. Baldridge

1936-39 – Charles R. Query

1939-40 – Lester N. Abel

1940-42 – Hugh W. Glenn

1942-46 – Carl Allinger

1946 – C.L. Hughbanks

1946-56 – W.A. Amerson

1956-59 – Dahlgren E. Casey

1959-66 – Lloyd Shannon

1966-77 – Richard Armstrong

1977-81 – Huie Holloway

1981-82 – Lloyd Sawyer (interim)

1982-98 – John Thrasher

1998-2000 – Mark and Becky Suter

2000-09 – Don Smith

2010 – Steve Seitz (interim)

2010-present – Tony Alstott

Endnotes

[1] Some of the material for chapters 1 and 2 are taken from the unpublished booklets "The Beginning of Methodism and a History of Wesley Chapel Church in New Albany, Indiana 1816-1954" and "Wesley Chapel United Methodist Church 'The Old Ship' 150 Years 1817-1967." The first booklet was written by Mrs. D.A. Smith, Ms. Katherine Cain, Mrs. Fred Jackson, Mrs. Louise Wolf, and Ms. Elizabeth Stoy. The second was put together in celebration of the 150th Anniversary of Wesley Chapel in 1967. The Church Historians who researched and wrote the history were Fannie Wolf, Helen Bence, Irma Mae Hublar, Florence Mann, and Hazel Long. Note that the original sources for this traditional account can be found in chapter 10 of the digitized History of The Ohio Falls Cities and Their Counties with Illustrations and Bibliographical Sketch at <www.archive.org/stream/historyofohiofal02will/historyofohiofal02will_djvu.txt> and C.W. Cotton's New Albany, Indiana, New Albany, 1873, 55-6 and in Biographical and Historical Souvenir for the Counties of Clark, Crawford, Harrison, Floyd, Scott, and Washington. John M. Gresham Company, 1889, 88-9. Shirley Kendall (former Wesley Chapel Historian) and Annette Gadlage are responsible for some of the material that was added to the unpublished booklet. Some notes by the Reverends W.A. Amerson, John Thrasher, and Tony Alstott also address the history of Wesley. References to these sources will simply be noted "Traditional History."

[2] US Department of the Interior National Park Service Registry of Historic Places, New Albany Downtown Historic District at <www.nafclibrary.org/Resources/Adults/Indiana/House/NewAlbanyDowntownHistoricDistrict.pdf>

[3] The descendants of Thomas Sinex, an early pioneer of New Albany, claim that he built the first "frame" house in New Albany. Sinex owned a lumberyard at Fifth and High Streets and donated material to build

the first Wesley Chapel Church on Lafayette Street between Market and Spring Streets. See Van Pelt, Bertha. October 13,1913. "Old Time Residents." New Albany Daily Ledger Standard. <www.nafclibrary.org/Resources/Adults/Indiana/ancestor/OLDTIMERESIDENTS.pdf> Van Pelt found 12 families who claim that their ancestors built the first frame or brick house in New Albany.

[4] US Department of the Interior National Park Service Registry of Historic Places, New Albany Downtown Historic District at <www.nafclibrary.org/Resources/Adults/Indiana/House/NewAlbanyDowntownHistoricDistrict.pdf>

[5] Mary E. (Wicks) Stoy. January 5, 1880. Obituaries. New Albany Daily Ledger Standard, 4

[6] Traditional History. According to Victor Bogle the house was owned by Hannah Ruff rather than Harriet Reynolds. See Bogle, Victor. A Society Develops in New Albany. Indiana Magazine of History. 49:2:June, 1953:173. Hannah Ruff appears in the "Story of Music" in New Albany Historical Series 3:24 at <www.nafclibrary.org/Resources/Adults/Indiana/History/Series/324StoryofMusic.pdf>. Cotton's account (Traditional History) cites Harriet Reynolds. The traditional account states that when Reverend Shrader organized the first Methodist Society on June 20 of the following year in the dining room of the hotel kept by Hannah Ruff.

[7] Traditional History. According to research by the Bicentennial Commission of the City of New Albany, the Union Church of New Albany and Jeffersonville first met on February 16, 1816. The following year it was renamed the First Presbyterian Church of New Albany. According to the Commission the first recorded Sunday School class was held in Hale's Tavern in 1817.

[8] See <geneaologytrails.com/ind/Floyd/obits/19=870.html>. Elizabeth Turner was the wife of Captain Henry Turner and passed away in 1872. According to the obituary of Elizabeth Turner, she and her brother

Obadiah Childs moved to New Albany in 1817 from Maryland. The narrative in this chapter places Obadiah in New Albany in 1816. See the Biographical and Historical Souvenir for the Counties of Clark, Crawford, Harrison, Floyd, Scott, and Washington. (John M. Gresham Company, 1889), 88-9. Turner's name appears on the Wesley Chapel Church Book as early as June 11, 1821 according to the obituary.

[9] L. C. Rudolph. Hoosier Faiths. Bloomington: Indiana University Press, 1995, 13.

[10] McGriff, E. Carver. Amazing Grace: A History of Indiana Methodism. Franklin: Providence House Publishers, 2001. 42-3. The restored version of the Robertson Meeting House or the Old Bethel Church can be found at Rivervale Methodist Camp.

[11] Baughman, John. "United Methodism in Indiana." Paper presented at the Inaugural Program of the Southern Indiana Conference Historical Society, DePauw University, April 27, 1996. <www.depauw.edu/library/archives/find/guides/umc_history/documents/sc000539fc.pdf>

[12] John Inglehart. "The Life and Times of John Shrader." Indiana Magazine of History. 17 1(March 1921): 2

[13] Wesley Chapel and the Indiana Conference recognize June 20, 1817 as the official beginning of the church. Reverend Shrader gave this account of the founding of Wesley Chapel while he was attending the Indiana Conference held in New Albany at Wesley Chapel United Methodist Church in 1871 (Traditional History). Note that June 20, 1817 was Friday, not Sunday and November 25, 1817 was a Tuesday, not a Sunday. This means that either the day or the date is incorrect as reported in this direct quote by Shrader. On the other hand, the other accounts that use these days do not mention the specific day of the week. It is possible that these events did not occur on a Sunday as Reverend Shrader's quote indicates. Just to further cloud the issue in the obituary of one of the founding members of Wesley Chapel, Mary Wicks Stoy, it states that the dedication of Wesley Chapel occurred on November 29, 1818 which was a Sunday. It also states that the

first prayer meeting was in the fall of 1817. Both of these dates are a year later than the dates given in the Traditional History. See the New Albany Daily Ledger Standard, June 5, 1880, 4. On December 7, 1817 the First Presbyterian Church of New Albany was also established (Traditional History). This church originated with the Union Church of New Albany, which started the previous year.

[14] Traditional History.

[15] See chapter 10 in the digitized History of The Ohio Falls Cities and Their Counties with Illustrations and Bibliographical Sketch at http://www.archive.org/stream/historyofohiofal02will/historyofohiofal02will_djvu.txt

[16] Traditional History.

[17] See chapter 10 in the digitized History of The Ohio Falls Cities and Their Counties with Illustrations and Bibliographical Sketch at <www.archive.org/stream/historyofohiofal02will/historyofohiofal02will_djvu.txt>.

[18] Thomas Sinex married Flora West in 1818 and both were life-long members of Wesley Chapel. He and his wife served on the Board of Trustees. In addition to being a successful lumber merchant, he served as an Associate Judge and was instrumental in the construction of the Court House in New Albany. His son, William, became a medical doctor and his son, Thomas H., became a Methodist Minister, the first President of Albion College, and President of the University of the Pacific.

[19] Presenting Flag and Flagpole. The Tribune. May 23, 1980, 2.

[20] McMurtrie, Henry. 1819. Sketches of Louisville. Louisville: S. Penn, Jun. Main Street, 168.

[21] Victor Bogle.

[22] Traditional History.

[23] Bogle, Victor. "A Society Develops in New Albany." Indiana Magazine of History. 49:2:June 1953:173.

[24] Lindley, Harlow. Indiana as Seen by Early Travelers. Indianapolis, 1916, 235.

[25] Collins, Mary Scribner Davis. "New Albany, with a Short Sketch of the Scribner Family." Indiana Magazine of History 17:3:September, 1921:224.

[26] Traditional History.

[27] Traditional History.

[28] John Bodger started the Indiana Cotton Manufacturing Company in New Albany in 1820. It was financed by several of the wealthier families of the town. The company made cloth but did not prosper and went out of business within a few years. See Bogle, Victor. "New Albany: A Flourishing Place." Indiana Magazine of History, 49:1:(March, 1953):15.

[29] Stoy was originally from Philadelphia and was a ship-cabin-builder in New Albany. He married Wicks on March 4, 1819.

[30] Items copied from a paper compiled by Peter R. Stoy and read at Wesley Chapel on February 8, 1885. Letter from Pam Peters (local historian in New Albany) to Bill Amerson.

[31] Traditional History.

[32] Traditional History.

[33] Traditional History.

[34] Traditional History. Note that the traditional history indicates that the original church on Lafayette Street burned down at some point in time.

[35] Traditional History.

36 Traditional History. See also IBID, McGriff, 47.

37 Traditional History.

38 Findling, John, ed. 2003. A History of New Albany. New York: Oxford, 53.

39 Traditional History.

40 Holliday, Fernandez C. 1873. Indiana Methodism. Hitchcock and Walden: Cincinnati, 124.

41 http://nafclibrary.org/wp-content/uploads/2016/07/SouvenirSketches-1.pdf

42 Fernandez C. Holliday, 10.

43 Thomas G. Beharrell wrote at least three books: The Brotherhood, Odd Fellows Mentor and Guide, and Lives of Eminent Bible Men and Women in Odd Fellowship.

44 Holliday indicates that "errors were committed in the early management of our denominational schools…[the school] did not rest on sufficiently solid pecuniary basis," 321.

45 Creason, Carl, Hannah O'Daniel, Katherine Gain, Daniel Michael, and Leanna Smith. Women Seminaries. <indyhist.iupui.edu/items/show/138>.

46 One source includes Peter Cartwright, Charles Holliday, William Shanks, and John Strange. See chapter 10 in the digitized History of The Ohio Falls Cities and Their Counties with Illustrations and Bibliographical Sketch at <www.archive.org/stream/historyofohiofal02will/historyofohiofal02will_djvu.txt>.

47 Life and Times of Allen Wiley, Indiana Magazine of History 23: 4: December, 1927: 435-39.

48 Rabb, Kate Milner, ed. 1840. A Tour Through Indiana in 1840: the Diary of John Parsons of Petersburg, Virginia, at <www.nafclibrary.org/Resources/Adults/Indiana/History/ATourThroughIndianain1840.pdf>.

49 Items copied from a paper compiled by Peter R. Stoy and read at Wesley Chapel on February 8, 1885. Letter from Pam Peters (local historian in New Albany) to Bill Amerson.

50 Traditional History. Church records at DePauw University indicate that between 1837 and 1843 membership of Wesley Chapel and Centenary stood at 943.

51 It should be noted that prior to this Wesley Chapel was known as the Methodist Church of New Albany. It was after it split with Centenary that it became Wesley Chapel.

52 Early Stoy Families.

53 Fernandez C. Holliday. Indiana Methodism at <archive.org/stream/indianamethodism00holl/indianamethodism00holl_djvu.txt>.

54 "Reverend James Hill, D.D." Northwestern Christian Advocate, September 10, 1902, 50:6.

55 Fernandez C. Holliday. Indiana Methodism at <archive.org/stream/indianamethodism00holl/indianamethodism00holl_djvu.txt>.

56 Will, Herman. 1984. A Will for Peace. Washington, DC.: General Board on Church and Society, 10.

57 Found in the New Albany City Directory, 1848 (NAFC Library Indiana Room)

58 Traditional History.

59 A Stranger's View of New Albany. January 7, 1852. New Albany Daily Ledger, at <www.genealogytrails.com/ind/floyd/newspaperarticles.html>.

60 Diary of Maria Graham 1851-56. Maria Graham Grant was a teenager in New Albany during the 1850s. Graham actually refers to Wesley Chapel as the "old ship" in her entry for August 1, 1855. See at <www.nafclibrary.org/Resources/Adults/Indiana/Peek/MariaGrahamDiary.pdf>.

61 Traditional History.

62 Traditional History.

63 Traditional History. It was suggested that perhaps the tradition of males sitting on one side and females on the other was discontinued because there were two center aisles in the new sanctuary rather than one.

64 Montagna, Douglas. "God Bless the Methodist Church: The Origins of the Methodist-Republican Alliance Before the Civil War." Methodist History. 54:2(January 2016):136-37.

65 Peters, Pamela. The Underground Railroad in Floyd County. Jefferson, NC, 2001. 14, 16-7. Also note that the Daily Ledger largely represented the interests of the Democratic Party whereas the other newspaper in New Albany at this time, the Daily Bulletin, largely represented the interests of the Whigs.

66 Pamela Peters, 55-8.

67 Dr. John Poucher, a member of Wesley as a youth and a Methodist Minister, delivered an invited address during the centennial celebration of Wesley Chapel in June 1917. He had attended Wesley during the 1850s and 60s. Comments about Crary were taken from his address to Wesley during the celebration. http://newspaperarchive.com/us/indiana/new-albany/new-albany-public-press/1917/06-26/page-5

68 Traditional History.

69 Dr. John Poucher http://newspaperarchive.com/us/indiana/new-albany/new-albany-public-press/1917/06-26/page-5

70 Emma Lou Thornbrough. The Negro in Indiana. Indianapolis, 1957. 45-6.

71 See Pamela Peters. She provides the best history of the Underground Railroad in New Albany.

72 Sketch found in John Warner Barber and Henry Howe Our Whole Country of the Past and Present of the United States, Volume 2, New York: Tuttle and McCauley, 1861, 1048.

73 Emma Lou Thornbrough, 185-6.

74 Arville Funk. The Morgan Raid in Indiana and Ohio 1863. Mentone, IN, 1971. 15.

75 Traditional History.

76 Theatre in New Albany www.nafc.library.org/Resources/Adults/Indiana/History/Series/217Theatre.pdf

77 Dr. John Poucher delivered an address during the centennial celebration of Wesley Chapel in June 1917. He had attended Wesley during the 1850s and 60s. See <newspaperarchive.com/us/indiana/new-albany/new-albany-public-press/1917/06-26/page-5>. See also Poucher, John. An English Colony in Floyd County. Indiana Magazine of History 11:3:211-15. Poucher and his wife Annie Cross had 8 children and seven of them graduated from college. <scholarworks.in.edu/journals/index.php/imh/articles/view/5939/5598>

78 Indiana Conference of the Methodist Episcopal Church. 1902. Minutes of the 71rst Session of the Indiana ME Conference. Cincinnati: Western Methodist Concern Press, 50.

79 Lipin, Lawrence M. Producers, Proletarians, and Politcians: Workers and Party Politics in Evansville and New Albany, Indiana 1850-87. Urbana: University of Illiinois Press, 1994.

80 Traditional History.

81 Smith, Wallace E. "The Reverend Stephen Bowers: Curiosity Hunter of the Santa Barbara Channel Islands." California History. 62:1 (Spring 1983) 35. After leaving Wesley Chapel, Bower became a self-made archaeologist and "collector of artifacts and geological specimens." His archaeological work in California was funded by the Smithsonian even though he used "questionable methods." He later became a newspaper publisher. His field journal The Noontide Sun: The Field Journal of the Reverent Stephen Bowers, Pioneer California Archaeologist was published in 1993. See also The Civil War Diary of Stephen C. Bowers by Glenn R. Schroeder, Indiana Magazine of History 79:2:167-85.

82 Bowers, Stephen, ed. "Reverend Stephen Bowers on Bower's Cave." Pacific Science Monthly. 1:1885:45-7 at <www.scvhistory.com/scvhistory/bowers1885.htm>.

83 His journal was published by Arlene Benson The Noon Tide Sun: the Journals of the Reverend Stephen Bowers, Pioneer California Archaeologist.

84 "Reverend Aaron Turner." Western Christian Advocate. January 20, 1897, p. 82

85 Traditional History.

86 New Albany Daily Tribune, February 22, 1872, 4:1 at http://genealogytrails.com/ind/floyd/obits1870.html

87 Lipin, Lawrence M. Producers, Proletarians, and Politcians: Workers and Party Politics in Evansville and New Albany, Indiana 1850-87. Urbana: University of Illiinois Press, 1994.

88 See <nafclibrary.org/wp-content/uploads/2016/07/SouvenirSketches-1.pdf>

89 Traditional History.

90 Lipin, Laurence M. Producers, Proletarians, and Politicians. University of Illinois Press, 237.

91 Lipin, Lawrence M. Producers, Proletarians, and Politcians: Workers and Party Politics in Evansville and New Albany, Indiana 1850-87. Urbana: University of Illiinois Press, 1994.

92 New Albany Daily Ledger, Jan 5, 1880, 4.

93 See chapter 10 in the digitized History of The Ohio Falls Cities and Their Counties with Illustrations and Bibliographical Sketch at <www.archive.org/stream/historyofohiofal02will/historyofohiofal02will_djvu.txt>.

94 Official Record of the Journal and Reports of the Annual Session of the Methodist Church, 305 — 06 at <books.google.com/

95 http://nafclibrary.org/wp-content/uploads/2016/07/SouvenirSketches-1.pdf

96 Traditional History.

97 A History of Clay County Indiana at <books.google.com/

98 Lipin, Lawrence M. Producers, Proletarians, and Politcians: Workers and Party Politics in Evansville and New Albany, Indiana 1850-87. Urbana: University of Illiinois Press, 1994.

99 Hodge, J. Vincennes in Picture and Story, 175 at <books.google.com/

100 Traditional History.

101 Traditional History.

102 New Albany Historic Districts — An Introduction (found in New Albany Design Guidelines, Introduction).

103 Herringshaw, Thomas William. 1904. "Vest, Emmons Rutledge." Herrinshaw's Encyclopedia of American Biography of the Nineteenth Century. Chicago: American Publishers Association, 963. At <books.google.com/

104 Reverend Emmons Rutledge Vest at <www.findagrave.com/cgi-bin/fg.cgi?page=gr&GRid=51791798>.

105 Indiana Church News, Western Christian Advocate, January 6, 1897, p. 27

106 Western Christian Advocate, June 30, 1897, p. 823, "Church News"

107 Smith, John L. 1892. Indiana Methodism. Northwest Indiana Methodist Conference: Valparaiso, 344. at <books.google.com/books?id=fz_

108 Bateman, Bradley. "The Social Gospel and the Progressive Era," Divining America, TeacherServ. National Humanities Center at <nationalhumanitiescenter.org/tserve/twenty/tkeyinfo/socgospel.htm>.

109 Western Christian Advocate, Indiana Conference, November 28, 1908, 24.

110 Western Christian Advocate, March 17, 1909, 28.

111 Traditional History.

112 Wesley Chapel Trustee's Report 1909-1910.

113 The Epworth League was created in 1890 and is the predecessor to the Methodist Youth Fellowship.

114 Traditional History.

115 Western Christian Advocate, January 7, 1914, 29 volume 80

116 Western Christian Advocate, August 26, 1914, 21

117 Traditional History.

118 Traditional History.

119 Western Christian Advocate, November 14, 1914, 1262 volume 80

120 Western Christian Advocate, "New Albany District" January 27, 1915, 92

121 Letter from Reverend O. E. Haley to Reverend Amerson. October 8, 1953. Courtesy of Bill Amerson.

122 Traditional History.

123 Norwood, Frederick A. 1974. The Story of American Methodism. Nashville: Abingdon, 2.

124 Moore, Leonard J. Citizen Klansmen: the KKK in Indiana 1921-28. University of North Carolina Press, 1997, 57-8.

125 Traditional History.

126 Traditional History.

127 Traditional History.

128 Interview with Warren Slider by Bill Amerson.

129 Letter to Reverend W.A. Amerson; also interview with Warren Slider by Bill Amerson.

130 Traditional History.

131 Phone interview with Emma Oldham in 1999. At the time she lived in the Mark Elrod Towers. Notes of interview are courtesy of Bill Amerson.

132 Letter to Reverend W.A. Amerson from Reverend Charles R. Query, September 22, 1953. Courtesy of Bill Amerson.

133 Ibid.

134 Traditional History.

[135] Letter to Reverend W.A. Amerson from Reverend Charles R. Query, September 22, 1953. Courtesy of Bill Amerson.

[136] "Abel, Rev. Lester." Indiana Obituaries A-F: Obitcity.com at <obitcity.com/indianaaf.html>.

[137] Wesley Chapel Women's Society of Christian Service, Secretary's Minutes 1940 — 1951. Courtesy of Bill Amerson.

[138] Traditional History.

[139] Letter to Reverend WA Amerson from Reverend Hugh W. Glenn, October 21, 1953. Courtesy of Bill Amerson.

[140] Reverend Carl Allinger, personal history (letter provided by his granddaughter Jacklyn Heeke). Courtesy of Reverend Tony Alstott.

[141] Ibid.

[142] Ibid.

[143] Traditional History.

[144] Wesley Chapel Women's Society of Christian Service minutes from 1940 to 1951. It is interesting and puzzling to note that besides the references to sending cards to the young men in the service, there is no discussion of WWII in the minutes. They met 3 days after the attack on Pearl Harbor and there is no mention of it. The minutes to the Society during WWI also contain no references to the war and there are no references to the hardships during the years of the Great Depression. These materials were provided by Bill Amerson.

[145] Reverend Carl Allinger, personal history (letter provided by his granddaughter Jacklyn Heeke). Courtesy of Reverend Tony Alstott.

[146] Traditional History.

[147] "Mid-Week Reminder." 3:36, September 5, 1956. Courtesy of Bill Amerson.

[148] Kruse, Kevin M. 1915. One Nation Under God: How Corporate America Invented Christian America. Basic Books: New York, 68.

[149] Materials provided by Bill Amerson.

[150] Obituary of W.A. Amerson, provided by Bill Amerson.

[151] "The Wesley Whirl." November 1949. Provided by Bill Amerson.

[152] Obituary of W.A. Amerson, provided by Bill Amerson.

[153] Traditional History.

[154] Traditional History.

[155] Traditional History

[156] Letter from Reverend Chester A. McPheeters to Pastor Amerson, February 8, 1954. Courtesy of Bill Amerson. The Metropolitan Methodist Church of Detroit was one of the largest Methodist churches in America at the time. There is a scholarship that is still offered by the church today in honor of Reverend McPheeters who was pastor from 1943 to 1957.

[157] "Mid-Week Reminder." 3:36, September 5, 1956. Courtesy of Bill Amerson.

[158] Traditional History.

[159] Cliff Staten, taken from a discussion with Virginia Shannon on Sunday, September 8, 2013.

[160] Letter to the congregation by Stella Newhouse dated February 19, 1962. Courtesy of Bill Amerson. Also Traditional History.

[161] Traditional History.

[162] The old pipe organ in the church was purchased by E.R. Cunningham of Fort Wayne, Indiana. Raymond Stoy, the great grandson of Peter and Mary Stoy (original members of Wesley) took several of the windows of the church.

[163] A typed copy of Bill Schuppert's talk was found in a scrapbook provided by Bill Amerson.

[164] Traditional History.

[165] Record Book of the Minutes of the Rebekah Circle of Wesley Chapel, 1966-1974.

[166] A Personal Testimony by Miss Stella Newhouse, June 1960. Document provided by Bill Amerson.

[167] Pastor's report to the Fourth Quarterly Conference, May 1, 1966. Courtesy of Bill Amerson.

[168] Conversation with Bill Amerson, 1/16/17.

[169] Will, Herman. 1984. A Will for Peace: Peace Action in the United Methodist Church. Washington, DC: General Board of Church and Society, 157-58.

[170] Traditional History. Interview with Warren Slider by Bill Amerson.

[171] This story was taken from an article from a newspaper that was in a church scrapbook put together by Fannie Wolf. The article had no date on it and I could not find the exact date but it was next to several articles dated late 1973 and early 1974.

[172] Traditional History

173 Gibson, Anthony. "Wesley Chapel Bids Fond Farewell to Pastor. Courier Journal. December 8, 1997, 12.

174 Ibid.

175 Traditional History.

176 Note written by Reverend Thrasher dated April 10, 1986. Provided by Bill Amerson.

177 A copy of the play was provided by Bill Amerson. Traditional History.

178 Traditional History.

179 Traditional History.

180 Documents provided by Bill Amerson.

181 Bussabarger, Kara. 2002. Searching for God. New Albany Tribune. March 3, 2.

182 Hollar, Barry Penn. US Methodism Deals with War and Peace at <www.mupwj.org/methodism.htm>.

183 Konick, Kris. "Wesley Chapel UMC-Life Cycle of a Building, Growth of a New Church." Banner Gazette. June 6, 2012, 91:26:2.

184 Esarey, Jenna. "Flock Breaks Ground on Floyds Knobs Site." Louisville Courier Journal. November 22, 2010, B1, B3.

185 Records of Wesley Chapel United Methodist Church.